Sarojini Bertha Peters

I was born in a happy, devout Christian home at Bareilly, India, on the 2nd of February. My parents named me Sarojini Bertha. Sarojini is a Sanskrit word for a lotus blossom, which is also the Indian National flower. In the early years, England had very few Christians. Bertha was one devout one. She was a queen, and greatly influenced the spread of her religion in South East England. I was named after her. I was educated at the Queen Victoria Girls High School at Agra, and continued at the Isabella Thoburn College, at Lucknow, India; receiving B.A., B.Ed.

I taught in Indian schools for a few years, before coming to London, England. I have had the great privilege to teach in schools of all ages and of all abilities. My greatest reward in my career was teaching the Partially Hearing Children.

I am now retired, and live in a comfortable home, with friendly neighbours and beautiful, quiet and peaceful surrounds.

Now and Evermore is lovingly dedicated to all who will care to read my book.

I dedicate my book to all my loving siblings, my family and to my beloved parents, late Rev and Mrs H.S. Peters; to my dearly beloved Mother, (step) late Dr Ruth Nora Peters, without whom I could not have been what I am today.

I dedicate *Now and Evermore* to all my dear friends, specially to Frances, Dorothy and Gregana whose coaxing encouragement made me materialise my life story. I thank them for their appreciation.

I do hope, *Now and Evermore* will be of some sweet joy and lots of laughter.

Sarojini Bertha Peters

NOW AND EVERMORE

AUSTIN MACAULEY PUBLISHERS™
LONDON • CAMBRIDGE • NEW YORK • SHARJAH

Copyright © Sarojini Bertha Peters 2024

The right of Sarojini Bertha Peters to be identified as author of this work has been asserted by the author in accordance with sections 77 and 78 of the Copyright, Designs and Patents Act 1988.

All rights reserved. No part of this publication may be reproduced, stored in a retrieval system, or transmitted in any form or by any means, electronic, mechanical, photocopying, recording, or otherwise, without the prior permission of the publishers.

Any person who commits any unauthorised act in relation to this publication may be liable to criminal prosecution and civil claims for damages.

All of the events in this memoir are true to the best of author's memory. The views expressed in this memoir are solely those of the author.

A CIP catalogue record for this title is available from the British Library.

ISBN 9781035819713 (Paperback)
ISBN 9781035819720 (Hardback)
ISBN 9781035819737 (ePub e-book)

www.austinmacauley.com

First Published 2024
Austin Macauley Publishers Ltd®
1 Canada Square
Canary Wharf
London
E14 5AA

Table of Contents

Introduction	9
The Beginnings	11
Schooling	27
Now and Evermore	46
The Wide World	52
England	60
Teaching and Retirement	82
Choirs and Clubs	95
Travel and Sights	102
Getting into Publication	126
My Selected Poems	138
My Love	138
The Sweetest Spot	140
England	142
Will No One Hear	143
To a Chestnut Sapling	144

The Lasers	**145**
Daffodils in a Vase	**147**
The Chosen Twelve	**148**
Easter	**149**
The Upper Room	**151**
Praise Thee	**154**
With Him Live…	**155**

Introduction

I was born in a deeply devout Christian home at Bareilly, India. It was here that the first American Methodist missionaries arrived in India in the mid-nineteenth century. Christian denominations had acquired vast areas in many cities in India, and Bareilly became the headquarter for the Methodists. Their work expanded, and in 1870, lady missionaries needed to come for medical work also to start education for girls; before that time, women could not be seen by a male doctor, and had no schooling. Thank God! How different things are now! Bareilly has the very first hospital for women founded by Dr Clara Swain. The hospital is now one of the best in India, if not in the whole world. Miss Isabella Thorburn started schooling girls from a small local group and expanded education for girls in India. First, a small school, then further developed to University level.

My grandparents lived in the latter decades of the nineteenth century. Things must have changed quite a bit by then. Methodism had made a big mark. My maternal grandfather was a Muslim, before he took on Christianity-a very difficult step to consider, as your own family didn't want to know you; facing all these hardships, he eventually became a Christian minister. Both maternal grandparents were lovely people taking an active part in Christian life. My paternal grandparents were formally Hindus, before seeing the truth. I did not see my grandfather, but my grandmother was deeply devout and prayed daily. Always telling us the love of Christ that she herself now knew.

It was these times when people denounced their old beliefs, religion, their way of life, taking up new culture and even new family names. Most Indian Christians have changed their names, though not necessarily to biblical ones.

When my grandparents accepted Christianity, my dad was a small lad. He went to Christian schools and after graduating from university, took on a high, lavishly paid post with the railways. But when he got the 'Call', he gave up his all to come into our Lord's service.

The Beginnings

Dad took a degree in Divinity and further studied Theology. He was ordained, and was appointed the Vice Principal and professor at the Theological Seminary, Civil Lines, Bareilly.

The Seminary covered a vast area outside the city, with three imposing buildings, beautifully kept lawns, scattered houses for the professors, and homes in line for married students, and a separate building for the bachelors, a kindergarten and a well looked after creche.

Our house – a bungalow was very near the first building, with a badminton court and our garden in between. The house had twelve or fourteen sprawling rooms, a wide veranda inside, a large walled-in courtyard and a wide veranda outside leading to our front garden.

Oh! Those were happy times living there.

We had two servants (helpers) in the house. One to prepare meals, see to the kitchen and the pantry; the other did the lighter chores around the house, like making beds, dusting, general tidying and laying dining table at meal times.

We were five siblings. All born of course at the famous Clara Swain Hospital. Catherine was first, then Emily, next was John, and I was not going to be outdone, so I came along.

Mercy still awaited her turn, and was born when I was not quite five.

We had a very happy family life. The day began when Dad got up first. He would start singing hymns of worship and praise. Among the most commonly he sang were:

Holy, holy lord God almighty; Fairest Lord Jesus, Nearer my God to thee! 'Rock of ages', and 'O Love that will not let me go'. He had a wonderful tenor voice; I remember him coming sometimes to wake me up before he had his shave, then tickle me with his bristled face saying, 'Daddy's Little darling will get up, will get up.' I laughed and giggled in his lap when he did his morning Daddy things! My mum was also an expert at spoiling and I should know.

When we were all waking up, getting washed and dressed, our breakfast was being prepared, brought to the table fully laid. He would then ring the bell to let us know. All of our four meals were family times. We all had our own seats. When we were all present, Dad would say a meal time prayer; it was not the usual, 'For what we were about to receive', but a full prayer, remembering the sick, the poor, the needy, all the friends and family, relatives and asking for gratefulness for the food and all His gifts of blessings. We had our main daily prayers at breakfast. Dad read a passage from the Bible and from a book of daily devotional readings. Sometimes, we sang hymns before the prayer was said.

Our food was simple, but wholesome. We helped ourselves, but I would not eat certain vegetables. Peas, potatoes and cauliflower were okay, but others, I would not touch. Dad would get me on his lap and say, "Daddy's little darling, a teenie bit." Nope! "Just a wee bit for dad." Nope! Then mum would take her turn. "Mum's sweet little one, a tiny bit." Nope! "Oh, your eyes will shine even brighter, if you eat your vegetables." The answer was still nope! All the fuss made over me fell flat. The little darling would not eat courgettes, pumpkins, gourd spinach and beet root.

Our dining was formal – proper use of cutlery, proper way of stirring tea, but stretching across the table, talking with our mouths full and elbows on the table never happened.

After meals, we went on doing our own things. I had stacks of toys in my playroom – all imaginable child's play. I had many dolls – rag ones, celluloid ones, china ones, wee ones, large ones, thin ones, fat ones, owning a sophisticated doll house fully fitted with furniture, china tea service, dinner service, little dishes; but to this little girl, dolls meant nothing. Not a pinpoint interest in them. I just could not see how I could say 'O, O little dolly go to sleep.' To me, it was just some substance rolled in the form of a doll. If at all, I spent quite a while with my china doll, but not because it was a doll; I was fascinated by its opening and closing eyes, and kept on making it do that over and over again, wondering how it really happened. My tiny brain could not work it out and to me it was a great marvel. All the dolls and all their possessions lay abandoned; I had absolutely no interest in them.

My best play things at that time were the two sets of stacking blocks like the Russian dolls. One with numbers and one alphabet. I liked making a tower with them. I liked feeling clever being able to do them in order, but then felt cleverer still when I'd stack them designing my own tower with a large box then quite a small one, then a large one and so on. It gave me quite a thrill, seeing my own creation. I was also quite fond of my set of buildings blocks. I would mount them in a tall tower, then topple them. The scattering and rattling enormously amused me. I kept on building my high towers and toppling them.

I was growing fast, and as soon as my two tiny feet started running around, nothing was there to keep me still. I soon started clambering on chairs and jumping off. In no time, the higher I could climb and the farthest I could jump, became an utmost thrill for me.

At about three years or so, I started Nursery School – a private one. A tonga, a horse carriage came to collect us children from our homes. The most I remember being there were my best sessions, when an apron would be put on us, and we were given some very soggy clay to play with.

I loved the squelch, through my fingers and the apron would be covered with splashes. We were also given large brushes and huge pots of paint to cover what we had created with the clay. I would take my big brush and plunge it into the red paint pot. The paint was everywhere but not where it was expected to be. My apron now covered with squelchy mud, dollops of red paint trickling like tiny rain drops. I would stand to show, hey! Look what I have done! O, yes! I also remember I had a boyfriend there! Real Prince, son of the Nawab. He and I got on really well.

Gosh! I laugh! I never had a prince charming; I never ever possessed those Cinderella shoes! But then I had a real prince for my friend.

By nearly four, I started the kindergarten, in the Seminary grounds and quite near our house. The kindergarten also had umpteen toys, but dolls and stuffed ones meant nothing to me. From this early age, the fascination of numbers had gripped me. They seemed, to have great magic about them; instead of the usual toys, most of the time, I spent was by the large abacus. It was higher than myself and had large colourful heads as the counters. I stayed on the abacus for a long time, getting more and more enchanted by the mystic numbers. When and if, I had the fill of the big beads, I'd get on to the building blocks. These were much bigger than the ones I had at home, so the clatter of the much higher towers toppling was thrilling, then the blocks were arranged to create the domino effect, in a straight line, curve or spiral which ever shape they were in with a little touch, and there! It all was not just amusing but deeply amazing! This fun kept happening again and again. I don't think I played with any other toy. Soon, it was time to go home.

Sundays were sacred for the family. They started as usual, Dad singing his hymns and the daily prayers. We had breakfast. I would then be dressed up to go to Sunday School which was held at one of the big rooms of the Kindergarten.

I liked going there. Our teacher, Mrs Franklin was lovely kind lady. She was the wife of the Seminary chauffeur, mostly wore a while sari, and had a huge chignon. After the Hellos, and Good Morning, we were seated on tiny chairs arranged in a moon crescent. I loved sitting directly opposite our teacher in the middle of the curve. She would begin with a short prayer, then we would join in saying the Lord's Prayer with our eyes shut and hands together. Next were the Bible stories like that of Samuel, the Prodigal Son and the good Samaritan, and we learnt to say relevant phrases or versus by heart, like *Lord, speak for thy servant heareth, and the Lord is my Shepherd, I shall not want.* We learnt to sing *choruses like, 'Give me oil in my lamp', 'This little light of mine'*. My love for singing started there, when I tried to sing loud trying to drown everyone else's voice. Some days later, I was extremely excited, when four of us were selected to sing a number at the main church for a special morning service. The central Methodist Christ Church is the second oldest Methodist church in India.

Its grounds are adjacent to the Seminary grounds and not far from our house. Our family attended all the services here; sometimes, Dad led a service, officiated at Holy Communion and solemnised several weddings. At this service, the four of us were to sing 'Lord make my life a little light; a little flower; a little song and a little rod on which the weak do lean.' My mum had dressed me in a beautiful pink chiffon frock, a huge pink silk bow in my hair, and I had new shiny shoes. When our time came, we were lined up in front of the packed church. We had to take a step forward to sing our verse in turn. Mine was the last; I stepped forward, raised my silver paper covered rod with a big pom pom, and sang as loudly as I could. It all went very well and I was mighty pleased with myself, when numerous 'well done, well done' followed.

At Sunday school, there were more Bible stories and more chorus singing. I loved them all but my best favourite was "Jesus loves me, this I know" singing it made me feel very special. Jesus loves me. How special is that! I never forget the most significant moment in my life. It was when we were told the First Miracle that Jesus performed in the Caana, of Galilee, I was listening with deep intent – something about Jesus Himself! I can still feel my jaw dropping and eyes bobbing the moment I heard of all that water turning to wine. A thud of amazement struck me – all that water turned into wine! And Jesus did it! I had barely recovered from the astonishment, when we were singing 'Jesus loves me.' This Jesus who turned all that water into wine loves me! How special is that! I felt more greatly special and more deeply loved. That moment became the firm foundation of the assurance of His great love for me. 'Jesus loves me,' this I do know and have always known. I would sing these words whenever and wherever I could, as loudly as my little lungs would allow. I sang with a deep sense of pride and certainty.

I was soon at the next stage – going to the Methodist Middle School for girls near the Seminary, across the main road. I liked it there. More magic of numbers and we started to learn to read and to write. We had small black boards to work on with a lump of chalk manageable by our tiny fingers. In the day during the class hours, we'd be taken out on to a large open ground surrounded by tamarind trees. There we would sing some group songs, play some group games, and sometimes sing and enact fairy tales. The best I loved was the story of 'Sleeping Beauty.' I was invariably chosen to be the princess as the children sang in a circle. My best bit was when the wicked witch had been and all the trees grew around me. Then of course the prince came clearing all the trees and waking me. We all sang and laughed.

A wonderful thing happened on the 4th of October.

Mercy arrived! Dad took me to see her at the hospital. I was thrilled having a teeny baby sister. She was a tiny bundle of delight utterly smothered with utmost sweetness and I dearly loved her and I still do. The best thing for me having Mercy at home was, that when in her baby pen, she'd leave some milk undrunk in her bottle; I'd ask mum if I could finish it. I would lie down beside Mercy and drink the bottle empty.

We had the Christmas holidays. Now, all the five of us. December ended; January passed, on the 2nd of February, I had my fifth birthday. School was still a lovely place to be in.

Time was rolling fast and it was soon the arrival of summer holidays. It was during these times that one day I was told mummy is going to Jesus. My mum is going to Jesus! Not yours, not yours, not yours, but my mum?! Jesus who loves me chose my mum to be with Him! How special is that! I was kind of elated, oh! For a child's mind! I did not quite understand what it really meant. I remember that day very vividly.

I was feeling great seeing so, so, so many people coming to see my mum when she is going to Jesus. The only puzzles were why mummy was still sleeping and why everyone was crying – they tell me not to cry when I do. I was puzzled by why they were not happy like I was. I don't think it really ever dawned on me what actually had happened. My dad's sister, Aunty Margaret came to see to us, and took great care of us. The school holidays were coming to an end. My two older sisters Catherine and Emily were already studying as boarders at a School in Agra. Dad decided that I should also go with them. But a problem occurred. I was just five, not old enough to be a boarder and the Principal pointed that. Little twisting of her arms and explaining the situation, I was accepted and became the youngest boarder at the Queen Victoria Girls High School.

I was very happy there, not at all daunted by the vastness of my new surrounds. It was also because, and I'm sure only QV would do that – there was a system that some older girls were given charge of the youngest ones to generally take care of them. These older girls were for the younger ones the school 'mothers'. My 'school mother' was my own sister Emily, and was there to see to my getting ready for school. After breakfast, we'd have a general inspection; the little girls lined up in the hall with their school mothers behind them. An appointed teacher came to see if we were properly ready for the day – nails clean, hair in place, shoes shining and frocks properly sashed.

I was thoroughly enjoying school work; we had started some elementary English. From my very early days, I was eager to be able to communicate in English. What with daddy's, "little darling", mum's "my sweet little one" singing choruses, reciting nursery rhymes, were all giving me a tremendous impetus to learn. I had loved stacking my little alphabet boxes and was enchanted by reciting. A for archer, B for bat, C for car, D for duck. I'd say the whole of it. But as I said the last three – X for xylophone, Y for yacht, Z for Zulu. I laughed and rolled about with a childish victory. Now at school, English and numbers were my greatest joy. To add to it all was our vast playground. We played Hop Scotch, skipping, organised rounders, running and racing.

For our work, we had weekly tests to keep an eye on our progress, then came the half-yearly exams, then the final year ending exams. Promotion on to the next year depended on these. I had already finished my first year, and now was in the second class, still doing well at learning. It was time for the half-yearly exams. I was over the moon when, just after these, I was promoted to the next class. First, I was the youngest boarder, now I was the youngest amongst my peers. More English and more numbers; we were reading good texts in English, and learnt the times tables up to twelve by heart. My favourite sums at this time were the LCM and the HCF. I wanted to be the quickest in doing them, and I was.

One day, my sisters told me that Daddy and Mummy were coming to see us. I very strongly rebelled, my mummy is with

Jesus. When I saw her from a distance, I rebelled even more strongly. She is not my mum, but on meeting me, she at once hugged me, cuddled me and kissed me. Just like my mum would have done. She got me on her lap. Plied me with sweets and more lovely things. I forgot all the differences and from that moment, she was my mum. And what a mum she was! Dad had remarried. We all were very young and needed a mother, and my darling step mother stepped in to fill the gap, fulfilling Jesus promise, "I will not leave you an orphan."

My mum was a medical doctor, drenched with super talents. At the end of the school term for the summer holiday, we came home to Dad and Mum. Happy days are here again! I absolutely loved my new mum, who wouldn't have! She was very loving, gentle, kind with fathomless patience, just what I, a stubborn self-willed spoilt brat needed. I was now eight years old, so no more of the building blocks; in fact, indoors did not suit me at all. I played outside in the garden catching butterflies, seeking out little worms or grabbing tiny baby frogs. I had learnt to skip and played Hop Scotch with my best chum – our gardener's daughter. I had also become a dense shadow of my brother John. Whatever he did, I had to do; wherever he went, I followed. He and I played marbles by the hours with our own formulated rules. I had become very fond of marbles. I'd rattle them in my pocket and count them over and over again to feel very rich, as marbles was my gold and treasure, my greatest riches! Then I'd go and win John's as well. I was the better of the two at our game. This was not, sadly, always the same though. At other times, I was not even included when John played cricket with his friends; and I was a total failure at handling a yoyo or flying a kite high in the sky, as I took the string off his hand, the kite would dash down, I'd give up.

If the kite did not stay up high, I myself loved climbing. The higher I could climb and jump from, the greater my delight. Climbing had become my passion. Just outside our front garden, was a neem tree. It was planted as a sapling by my grandfather, so my grandmother told me. Its trunk before it forked into branches was a bit out of my reach, but John could climb it. If John climbed the tree, I also just had to. With my stubborn tantrums, he was forced to help me get up there. He would crouch, get me on his shoulders and stand up. I would then clamber as high as I could go, higher and higher the deeper my thrill. Danger was not the faintest fancy. When John wasn't there to assist me; poor Bobby, our dog had to suffer. He'd be sitting on his cane chair on the veranda, I'd go, get him up. "Bobby, get off; Bobby, get off!" Poor thing! He'd surrender. I would then pull his chair out by the tree trunk and be up in my glory. The neem tree had become the love of my life!

This was a great dismay for Dad. He tried to discourage me in many ways. He tried to explain the danger of how I could fall and break my neck or cripple myself or have to spend days in the hospital. But danger was inconceivable. Nothing of my Dad's explaining was working. He was losing every time. He tried other ways and one of his tricks actually worked! but even that didn't last for long. He asked me to get him some water to drink. I was a bit surprised, asking me for a glass of water! When I did bring it and he drank it, he then piled me high of praises. How Sweet The water was, how lovely the nectar brought to him by his little darling, I was absolutely chuffed flattered, the water I bring for Daddy is so sweet. Little did I know of his cunning! Every time he sensed I was nearing the tree, he'd become very thirsty, and call his little darling for the sweet nectar, water. Once he'd drink it and piled me high with flattery, he'd find other little things to keep me occupied beside him. But once he was loosened, there, I'd be back on my tree.

Dad had also had a swing put on one of the thick neem branches. The rope made of leather was long and the swing pendulum was wide and high. For me being on the swing or climbing had become parallel. Sometimes, if not climbing or swinging, some of us neighbouring children also played a game on one of the trees that were lining the wide path from the main road to our house. The rules of this game were our own invention and were similar to playing "Hide and Seek". The blind man was chosen by doing eenie meenie, or by pulling a leaf with a notch. This game with our own intricate rules was played for hours. Tiredness we did not know what that was. If It was rainy or stormy and we could not play outside, John and I were homebound. We had several table games – Dominoes, playing cards, Draughts were ok but we mostly played Ludo or Chinese Checkers but the little shiny, glittering marbles on the walnut board mostly excelled. Most of our time was spent in the drawing room playing with these marvellous marbles on the walnut board. Of course, I won most of the time!

After dinner, Mum and Dad played Lexicon; a card word game forerunner of Scrabble, while John and I played "Word-making – and taking", a children's word game. Small lettered tiles faced down were arranged in a circle, upturned one by one in turns. As soon as a word was spotted, it was taken as yours and whoever had the most words at the end, won. I was still at the stage of knowing three or four letters words, but to my childish brain, that was a lot. One day, I challenged Dad to play Lexicon, "Dad, I want to play Lexicon with you." "Oh no, no," was his answer, "You have to know a lot more words to play lexicon with me." He said. Well, that really did it!

From then on, any long word I saw or read, I tried to learn it. In our dining room was a plaque that read 'Christ is the Head of this house. An unseen guest at every meal and the silent listener of every conversation.' I could not read or comprehend it. The word 'listener' puzzled me. What could lis.ten.er be? The ten I thought was the number ten. I was trying to be really clever. I broke the word 'conversation' into syllables. It became con.ver.sa.tion. Now I could very easily spell a long word. Well, surely now I am well equipped to play Lexicon with dad, I was proudly certain. So, I challenged him again after a few days. Dad complied this time. "Well come on then," he said. I was as happy as I could be playing Lexicon with Daddy. And guess what! Poor boy! Kept playing two or three letter words and I was putting my three or four letters down. Then I came up with my ace, a six-letter word, 'parrot'. Dad deliberately had let me win. My thrill knew no bounds. I was telling everyone, even the outsiders who happened to pass by our house, as loud as I could yell, "I beat Daddy at Lexicon!" The thrilling experience made me more and more intent on learning new and long words. Dad had played his cunning trick on me and this time, he really won. Words became my great fascination like the numbers.

At home, mum was doing wonders. In season she would make fruit jams, apple preserves; her guava jellies were absolutely yummy. She made them so expertly; you could not buy like that in any big shop. Her pickles, chutneys and ketchups were also matchless. My mum had magic hands, I'm sure. She actually proved it to be true. Many of our clothes were stitched by our family tailor. He'd be sent for, he'd take the material and in a few days, he'd bring the newly made dresses for our delight. As usual, Dad took us to the shop to choose our material. Both Mercy and I liked one specially the best. We expected the next morning our tailor would come and in a few days, we'd have our new pretty dresses. But, the very next morning instead of the tailor coming, to our tremendous surprise, we already had our most beautifully made dresses with pretty patterns. We both were excited. Our darling mum had sat in the night making them to give us this amazement and utmost delight. Has anyone else ever done that? I wonder.

Life was sailing smilingly. My sisters Catherine and Emily were in Agra without me this time. I attended the Methodist Girl Middle School as a day scholar with both Mum and Dad at home. I liked the school for the things we learnt and did there. Among the times I enjoyed very much were, our weekly assembly. The last period every Wednesday, we'd take our places in the hall; this was more of a show when every class had to put on a skit or two; perhaps enact a part of a lesson or sing a special song, or if someone had written a good essay or so. I loved taking part in this. I was especially proud when I was chosen to recite a short poem. "Cocks Crow in the morn, to tell us to rise". Nursery rhymes had already made an impact on me. My most favourite was "Jack and Jill." In my younger days, I'd be saying it any or everywhere.

I used to be puzzled, why Jack was wearing a crown?

I thought only kings wore one. I was also amused thinking "Fe" was one word and "tchapail" (fetch a pail) another. This made me feel I was saying a clever long word! And Jill and hill sounded quite lovely. I think what an enchanting style of writing poems and rhymes is. A simple thought expressed with such floral flourish!

The days were passing rapidly. My dad was suffering from diabetes. Mum being a doctor took care of him, but it was painful to see him getting injections every day before meal times. I was now in the final year of the middle school; soon I was to take final external exams set by the government. I sat my exams and the results would be out in a few weeks' time announced in the National newspaper. In this duration, Dad had been given a transfer. This was very bad news for me. It would mean leaving our lovely house, my beloved neem tree and the long swing, the vast playing grounds, our badminton court, the tennis court, the beautiful lawn and the tree on which children played our own game. It all was going to be a tough wrench.

The only pacifying thought was getting into the newness of everything.

Dad was appointed District Superintendent, next to the Bishop. He'd have the church work of several districts under his supervision. Our house in Muzaffarnagar was literally attached to the church and as I expected, not as big as our bungalow. Still big enough, with several rooms, a wide veranda and a vast walled in courtyard. At least I had found one delight! Like most houses in India, ours also had a flat roof with a wide stairway to go up to it. Yes, I climbed up and down it as much as I wanted to. I found another outlet for my fidget. Seeing my sisters in Bareilly riding a bicycle given to them by my uncle, I also wanted to ride, but my legs could not reach the pedals. In my frustration I'd throw up a tantrum. I wanted to ride the bike. My dad, to appease me, would get me on the seat and take me round and round on the tennis court. Now with the large courtyard, my stubbornness played up. I just had to ride the bike. I got it out and legs still not long enough, I put myself on the carrier at the back and tried to ride all by myself and no help. First, a few feet, then a few more. I was well taming the bike it was now under my control. Every few more feet and I was excited. By the third day of my efforts I was well accomplished. Bursting with excitement I called out, 'Daddy, daddy come and see me, I'm riding the bike.' Dad was stunned and very pleased with my achievement. From now on, I was Daddy's little darling and his adventurous one, as well!! I now had the stairs and the bike to keep me occupied. I spent much time riding the bike in the courtyard or out in the wide Church grounds. Do you know I never ever once fell off my bike!!

One day when the newspaper was delivered, it had my middle school results. To everyone's joy and my excited delight, I had passed my exams and passed well with distinction in Arithmetic. My parents and everyone was proud of me.

By now, having finished schooling, Catherine was training to be a teacher and Emily was attending the Christian Medical College at Ludhiana. For me to continue, without my sisters all by myself, I'd be back to Agra.

Schooling

To this day, I cannot tell, I do not know what made it so wonderful. I always felt I was in a Fairy Land. I felt every inch and every second was too short at this school – The Queen Victoria at Agra. I do not know whether it was the trees, flowers and the marvellous buildings, their locations or the ground surrounding them. I just so loved it all. The school was established in the late nineteenth century by the Church Missionary Society with the Church of England. It is renowned for the high academic standard and firm Christian teaching. Although Dad was a big name, Rev Professor Peters and highly revered and regarded in Methodist Church and outside, he was also strong and passionate advocate for the unification of churches. God loves everyone the same. Dad wanted us to know that, so instead of attending a Methodist school, all of us were boarders at the Queen Victoria Girls High School. We all were confirmed in the Church of England.

The main entrance to the vast three-storey building was in the north leading through a wide corridor into a huge hall, then the south veranda connecting the dining hall and the kitchen. From here, an open but covered corridor led into the washrooms. All classrooms were located on the ground floor.

An enchanting spiral staircase led to our living accommodation above the huge hall. Thirty-two beds, eight in each quarter of the dormitory, and few on the East and West verandas. I loved sleeping in and was quite mesmerised by the high ceiling and the wide doors and windows on either sides. In the morning, a bell was rung indicating time to get up. We ran down the spiral staircase, through the two verandas, the open corridor, to the washrooms. When we were all washed and ready, a special bell, used only for prayer time, was rung and we'd have 15 minutes of quiet time. We read our Bible and said our prayers, each girl by herself.

Time for breakfast, and the spiral staircase – thrilling running round and round what fun!!! Each step wide on side, narrow in the centre. The dining hall had nine large tables arranged in three long lines. We all had our own seat. Each of our four meals began and ended with a sung Grace. The most usually opening one was "Look on the hungry Lord, we pray. Supply our needs from day to day. Upon our souls Thy spirit pour, that we may love Thee More and more." We ended with, "Thank you for the world so sweet, thank you for the food we eat, thank you for the birds that sing, thank you, Lord, for everything." Our dining was formal. We all had our own seat. Tables were set and food was laid out in big dishes and platters. We could eat as much or as little as we wanted. In theory we helped ourselves, but to make it easy, a senior apt girl opted to serve. I absolutely loved our school food, and literally ate quite a lot! But of course, vegetables were a big 'no' for me. The senior head of our table was Ruth Mull. I'll never forget her. She offered vegetables to me but I'd say 'no', so it was ok. One day Ruth Mull happened to be near me when I was reading my daddy's letters.

In it, he had said his usual 'darling, be good, study well, take care of yourself, and the tough order, "Eat your vegetables!" Ruth Mull grabbed the letter from my hand and said, "Let's see what your dad has to say." What audacity, but then this was Ruth Mull. Reading the line, 'eat your vegetables did it.' The next day serving food at lunch, and in spite of my big 'no', Ruth plonked a huge lump of some detested vegetable on my plate, adding, "Your dad says eat you vegetable, you must." I was stubborn, I wasn't going to eat. She insisted strongly, but I wouldn't budge. I hadn't realised I was dealing with a gendarme Ruth Mull. The meal ending grace had been sung, all the other girls left the hall. But I was in this cage. Ruth with her arms on her hips, "eat that bit on your plate," her eyes glaring, school bell was about to ring, I even started crying, "I do not want to eat this lump." Ruth wasn't to move. Finally, my stubbornness yielded. Somehow, I actually swallowed that mound. This happened again and again, until I discovered, I really liked those vegetables. What a miracle! I eating vegetables! Where Mum and Dad's sweet pleas had failed, gendarme Ruth's glaring eyes had succeeded. Now, those very vegetables – pumpkin, gourd, courgettes, brinjals (aubergines), I eat with such relish and say a grateful thanks to Ruth Mull, and so wish my beloved parents were here to see me eat those greens. All the meals were now food glorious food, vegies included. Dining hall a big winner.

The classroom also had great enchantment for me.

All our lessons were in English. A big step closer to my childhood zeal of being able to communicate in English. To add to that, a delicious addition to our lessons – Mathematics. I loved every line, every square, circle, every triangle; from whichever angle I looked at it, each degree made a point on me, with all the English Arithmetic and Mathematics, how could I not be happy? O, but there is always a damp pedal and this was History. I did not want to know what the battles were, where they were fought and who and why they fought. I wasn't concerned if Henry had five, six or sixty wives, whom he loved and whom he killed. Not my concern. I couldn't care to know Shah Jahan built the Taj Mahal in 1666, the same year as London was burning down to ashes. The Taj could have been built by Tom, Dick or Harry; what did it matter to me? I did not know who Shah Jahan was, I never met him! None of all this was my concern.

If History was a no, no, sewing was an unsurmountable mountain miles, miles beyond me. Every lesson, thankfully just once a week, started with a bawl, 'I can't do it'. This was well and truly proved to be so, when our sewing packs were handed out, my needle decided playing a disappearing act, literally in a hay stack. I searched and searched high and low for it, finally I did find it. Now to thread it, I got the cotton from the reel, but that had spun itself into a massive spider's web. Try again and again. Success at last! the Cotton is straight and the needle threaded, but the knot at the end is more like a tennis ball, than a tiny knot. With all this I'm already quite miserable, only further to realise that the material I'm supposed to stitch is all awry. Why, oh why? even Darwin's Theory refused to work on me? I desperately needed another pair of hands to evolve. No evolution on me; I just had to get on with my two helpless hands. Somehow, I managed to get the things together and stitched at least an inch or so, only to discover I had stitched my skirt with it also. So unravel the stitches and whole saga all over again. By the end, my poor painful finger had become the envy of a well-furrowed field, with all the digs I had from the needle, even with not much real sewing done. Blissfully, it was time to pack up. Every lesson ended drowned in pools of spools of tangled tears and no hope. To this day when a blouse loses its button it is thrown into redundancy, or a safety pin proposes to come to its safety and rescue. My deepest commendations are for people who can stitch and create such beautiful things with cross stitch, runner stitch, this stitch and that stitch. My mind boggles and, I consider all these amazing people to be the greatest genii of the human race.

Thankfully, sewing was just a part of Domestic Science which included hygiene and physiology and First Aid. These were enough to make up for my inadequacy in sewing. I enjoyed happily learning the names like cerebrum, cerebellum, ventricle, phalanges, patella, intestines; all were well digested. I also always offered my services to be the badly hurt victim, when we had our first-aid lessons. The rest could practice doing the 'figure-of-eight' bandage and the arm-slings on me. Helplessly, I wasn't a shine in Urdu either. Its script was my slide. I always managed to get the loops and the dots in the wrong place. All through the schooling, I could never get the hang of it. In my consideration, Urdu is a very beautiful language. Well-spoken, it sounds very sweet, regal and extremely polite. Urdu poetry would melt any one's heart.

Class work on the whole was enjoyable and then there were the games to look forward to. I could not wait. Jumping about and leaping sky high. That was I! Games were the love and soul of my life. I never wanted them to end. I loved playing most games and I was good at them. I played Deck Tennis, Badminton, Volleyball but my most favourite was basketball. It seems the rules of the game have changed, but we played with six on each team – two defenders, two centres and two shooters (scorers). I was the shooter. Whenever possible. I was on the court sometimes all by myself, dribbling the ball from one post to the other and into the basket. I had even discovered a theory for myself. If I hit the ball on an imaginary perpendicular from the base of the ring, the ball was sure to go in through the basket. Those who play basketball try it; it will always work; I guarantee.

Our games attire was whiter than snow. Keds (tennis shoes) with matching socks, and whiter than white blouse and a blue tunic. We all looked elegant. At the end, a bell went for us to stop playing and get into the classroom for the evening study. Shhh! I was a very naughty girl! All the girls went in, not I! I kept on having as good a time as I could with my ball, when the spoilsport study teacher came out to tell me to stop playing and get in. Just then, with all naughty deliberation, I'd kick the ball the farthest and pretended it happened by accident. How very naughty a school girl can be! Study? I did not want to know. Yet all good things do come to an end. For me, a bit too soon. The Marker came to collect the equipment, and I most unwillingly give up, also, I didn't want to be missed too much at my empty desk in the classroom.

Time was passing fast. I was now a full 12 years old. In spite of my being so playful, my school work was passable. I did well in my half-year exams. Towards the end of the final term, one day I felt a bit feverish and was sent to the Sick-Room. In the morning, breakfast was brought up, but before I could get to eat it, I felt a massive shiver; I was shaking like a tiny twig in a rattling storm. I fell in a deep coma. This was a bout of malaria. I was running a very high temperature 106.4.

I lay in the bed the whole day. Later in the evening, when I came round and opened my eyes, I heard a happy cheer around me. They had been giving me continuous cold sponges all the way. I was taken to the main hospital to make a full recovery. I did, and soon was my strong and sturdy real self again. My parents were concerned, so they took me home. This meant I missed the final end of term exam. The general class work buttressed me, and I was put into the next year.

Things were happening as merrily, happily as always. I was loving QV as much as I had from the start with beautiful buildings, lessons, games and all the food. Soon, it was time for holidays and I was home for Christmas. As for everyone, this was a very special time of the year with all the decorations, Christmas tree, presents and yummy goodies. But in spite of all the jollity we had a down side. Our beloved Dad was looking more frail. With all the available medicines and care, he was not getting over his illness. Christmas happened and then New Year and it was time for Agra again.

This time, I was a bit sad seeing the way our Dad looked. Still, in my wildest dream, I hadn't dreamt that this would be the last Bye Bye; Dad's last kiss and his last "Dad's little darling". At school, I was being my usual. Detesting History, incompetent at sewing, lapping all Maths and jumping about and leaping sky high in the games ground. And so, January passed. On Sunday, 2nd February was my thirteenth birthday. I was very happy. They all sang for me at breakfast, and I received many beautiful cards and lovely presents from the girls. At my Dad's request, our Principal said a special prayer with me, and wished me a 'Happy Birthday'. I was very excited with my feathers well ruffled. I was now a fully-fledged teenager. I continued to be wished well for my big day.

Two weeks later on Saturday, the 15th, our Principal came to our dormitory; the most unusual thing ever to happen. She came directly towards me and called me. I was absolutely jolted. What had I done? Where had I gone wrong? That my Principle herself should come for me. The only calming was that her voice was soft and kind. Her placid talking of everything but my crime wasn't the faintest hint. I just wasn't getting it. She led me to her room, kindly offered me a seat, and handed me a letter from my uncle, telling me that our beloved Dad had passed away. Dad died on Sunday, the 9th exactly a week after my birthday. Everyone was gentle and very sympathetic towards me.

Having lost our dad, now our father, mother, guardian shelter all rolled into one. A single, widow, stepmother, what do you say to that? What a shelter? What a guardian? What a mother? All this on her shoulder. She never moaned, she never complained and sweetly supported us firmly in every way, all on her own. She now had to get on to work. My mum was appointed as a Supervisor of the Methodist Medical work in Bengal. Mother was stationed in a place not far from Kolkata. Here was a wide Christian following, with two big Mission schools, a small hospital, separate medical dispensary and a church in vast open ground, surrounded by many mango trees. In December, trees would be loaded with fruit and gee! We had our fill all summers holiday!

I still had two and a half years of school, so back to books. In my final years, Yippie, I got rid of that horrid History, but that stressful sewing was still strongly stitched on me. Same tragic tears! To compensate for the lachrymal, lucious lollies were added to Maths; we now also had Logarithms and Trigonometry, so we had lessons more often in the week. I enjoyed them all but why did they end so quickly!!

Apart from our general lessons, we also had Scripture study throughout school. The courses and exams were set by the Diocese. Mondays and Thursdays, New Testament; Tuesday and Fridays, Old Testament and on Wednesday, we studied the Prayer Book. I was happy and grateful for these to widen my knowledge and strengthen my faith. Our school day began with a Chapel service. In the evening, we boarders had our vespers. Sundays were sacred. We attended city churches, morning and evening. and the weekly Lent Services. A hymns practice was on Saturday, of course, singing was my great joy. We had several other activities to attend to. Besides games every week, there was 'Guides' with group games, and singing songs like 'Row, row, row your boat', 'Kookaburra sits on an old gum tree' and 'There were three jolly fisherman', all quite hilarious. But I was all knotted up when it came to doing the knots. I was an expert doing the granny knot and the reef knot superbly perfect each time. Can you match that?

One of the great days in the school Calendar was the 'Old Girls Day' to remember girls from former days. Some of the 'old girls' who could come, came and we had special service of Thanksgiving for them. Some had written letters remembering their happy times. Their epistles were read out. In the evening, to continue the celebration, we had informal games, various races, and no guessing who won the high jump prize!

Another very special date on the calendar was our Prize-Giving Day. A grand show was put on for all the outside invited guests. I loved being in the pretty song numbers. We did not have a set school uniform but red and white were the school colours. We all wore them one way or another. My white frock had red piping on the hem, on the collar and on the wide sash. We all felt great prancing around in our colours. With that, I also had to recite a long poem titled 'Voice and Vision'.

After it's long wear and tear, our school needed a new bus, and efforts were made to raise funds for its replacement. A play 'The King of the Golden River' was rehearsed and prepared for a grand evening for people to come and see. I was glad to be in the play and acted as the main character, 'Gluck', the youngest of the three brothers, affluent, yet shy of sharing their abundance with others. The show went off with a great success, and we had our bright, grand new school bus.

My other cherished memories of the wonderful school days are when we were taken out on excursions. We had half day school on Saturday, and the first Monday of every month was a holiday. Picnics were arranged and we visited all the fabulous landmarks in Agra-the Mughal capital of India; we visited the amazing Taj Mahal, Sikandra, Fatehpur Sikri and the Fort. Picnic in the grounds of these enchanting venues was quite some experience.

All good and wonderful things have to end. My super school days were no exception. Final exams were knocking at the door. These were set by the government and the results would be announced in a few weeks' time in the National newspaper. This would also mean to pack up my belongings for the last time and leave my perfect paradise, my haven of havens. It was a great pain to say goodbye to my so-loved

Queen Victoria Girls High School at Agra – the grand city of the Taj Mahal.

Few weeks passed, and our results were in the papers, and as I had expected and knew for sure with my inadequacy and incompetence, what else could be the outcome? *All the kings horses and all the kings men* could not stop me from falling. I had fallen flatly, flatter then flat, failed. If sewing was miles miles beyond me, I was miles and miles behind my class and exam assignment. I am quite happily prepared to declare, it must be far easier to make a crack in the Himalayan Rock than to stitch a button on my button less frock. Of course I failed this stressful task, but was loyally pulled high up by the others, and happily, over all, I passed and passed well with two distinctions, one in Arithmetic and one in Mathematics.

My school results opened up gates for further higher studies.

My darling Mum, was there anyone else like her out there? I wonder! always wanting the best for us, made an application for my admittance at the Isabella Thorburn College in Lucknow. The college is famous for its high academic standards and for being the top and the best women's institution in Southern Asia. The Principal was highly authoritative and deeply revered, also from being the first Indian, and the first lady to be one of the Presidents of the World Council of Churches. (One year the council was held on the college campus). With QV education and two distinctions, I was excited to be accepted as a student, but there was a hitch. The lowest age to be a boarder was sixteen, I still had a few months to reach that goal. That was the hitch for me to be a resident scholar. My mum insisted what else would I do if not be studying. Our Principal suggested that I should stay at a nearby YWCA and cycle to college every morning. My mum caught her on that, 'Yes, she is old enough to cycle on those dangerous roads but not old enough to be a resident in the college.' That did it. I was the youngest boarder at the Isabella Thorburn College. I was delighted; I also started receiving three very generous scholarships.

The new students had to register a week before the actual classes started. This Orientation Week was meant to familiarise the new ones with the college routine. The daytime was used for aptitude and IQ test. I passed these quite happily and was well prepared for the new life in this entirely new world.

American lines prevailed – we were Freshman (freshies) Sophomores (sophs) and Junior and Seniors. We had semesters and vacations. Everywhere else also, there were American touches that made it all feel exotic and glamorous. Most beautiful grounds with well-kept garden, lawns, a huge fountain in the centre and sidewalks lined with flourishing flowers. My favourite spots were the flower garden and the adjacent rose garden. I often drifted into them to cut my fill of highly-scented carnation, nigella, and roses. Yes, we could cut blooms from here but elsewhere we were warned. 'Roses are not flowers.'

Exotic roses adorned the sidewalks – highly tempting! Lupins were new to me, I stood there for a long time admiring them for their shape and gentle hue.

Wow! Wow the vast playing fields. Just the thing for me. Hockey, Soccer, Baseball and Tennis courts all included in the ground, holding the other games as well. I wasn't quite hit by soccer, hockey or even tennis but threw in my lot happily playing the other games. I was always ever ready for badminton, basketball and volleyball. One year, the Government arranged Inter-College Volleyball tournament. I was on the college team. It was most exciting. We had to travel overnight by train to Allahabad. Arriving there, we slept at the premises, and in the morning, all refreshed to face the game. It was a hard match and, argh, our team lost. At least we had played our best, and seen a new place. Back at college, every one greeted us with 'well done' and cheers. That was enough to pacify. Next morning, the national newspaper had a write up on the game, naming every player to say how they had done. Someone said to me, "Hey, you are famous! Your name is in the newspaper." I rushed down to the Social Room to see it for myself. There it was! My name in the National newspaper! All the sorrow of losing the match was lost. I felt I had conquered the world! Deep sigh of joy perhaps! Turning the page over, I was absolutely awestruck. There was a page size picture of the newly opened Royal Festival Hall in London. Its lavishness cast a strange striking spell on me.

Formal games were a wonderful aspect of college life. Games were strictly compulsory. We wore navy blue gym suits and white Keds. My favourite game was Basketball and I was a shooter. I could never have enough of it and you must blame the game, as while at it, once again I became the school girl not wanting to leave the grounds. Game time was over; all the other girls left but I was still with that ball all on my own. I could go on playing, this time; no teacher to come to tell me to stop and get into study. Sometimes, it was quite late until the spoil sport Marker came to collect the equipment and I, most reluctantly, handed him the ball.

The highest height of our games program was our Sports Day. That created quite a thrill of excitement. In preparation for the great day, primary matches were played over several days, classes against classes, the three halls of residence against each other, and even the Professor's team played against students. There were banners to be made and cheer slogans rehearsed.

On the day itself, final matches were played. All the cheering in the air created a festive atmosphere. There were informal games also. All my ability of climbing trees and playing basketball had not made me a good runner, so I stayed out of any involving pure running. I then threw in my lot at the javelin throw, and won prizes both for style and distance. I had my highest contentment.

In July and August on very hot evenings, instead of court games, we had swimming in a large pool with both shallow and deep ends. This was another totally new experience for me, but of great fun. Perhaps from being an Aquarian, I soon took to water, and in no time, I learnt to keep myself floating. I remember a day very vividly when the world swimming champion couple was with us. They demonstrated some of the most intricate moves in the water. Watching them was amazing. What a feat!

The games grounds had another very strong attraction for me. It happened late in the evening after dinner when the full moon was out. I would go there all on my own, drowned in gleaming glory, the vastness surrounding me and the moon my canopy. At the farthest end of the vast openness, was my fascination – the eucalyptus grove. I would drift into it. There, the all silvery trunk of tall trees – the golden glimmering leaves created a magical magic around me, enhanced by the sound of the crumpling leaves under my feet, and the rustling of the tangled twigs. I was in a new amazing world and wanted to linger on and on. It was all so very wonderful, but it would soon be time for the night watchman to come, and with the fear of being mistaken for an intruder and be charged at, I'd leave. My friends still wondering where I had been while I was roaming in a magical land of my dreams.

College life was an ocean of rich experiences. It was a great privilege to be submerged in it. I had always loved singing. We had auditions to form three different choirs. The smallest one sang specially for our Sunday morning service held in our very beautiful chapel built of white stone and quite away from the other buildings. Inside, a marble altar under a stained glass window; heavily carved pulpit and large brass eagle-shaped lectern above which hung a filigreed lamp, the light of which was never dimmed or switched off, to symbolise Christ's Eternal Light. The lamp is the college emblem. Choir pews were next to an electric Hammond organ, which was played by our director, Music graduate from Julliard, New York. Singing most beautiful anthems to the resounding sound of the organ, was the most uplifting experience. The evening choir included some outsider, gentlemen to form a full score. We were the City Central Methodist Church Choir. Our music director was the church organist. Excerpts from great works were sung as Anthems.

Special choral works were sung at Christmas and Easter services. The church was decked with seasonal décor – red and green poinsettias and others at Christmas, and spotless white lilies at Easter. It was a joy to sing in a church full to capacity. After the Christmas carol service, we'd be taken to the All India Radio Station to have our singing recorded. It was great fun listening to ourselves later on. We also received several congratulations from people who heard us over their device.

The third choir was the Concert Chorus. It included some non-Christian girls, as well. We sang on special dates like the Founder's Day. This was celebrated with great aplomb. Activities started in the morning and culminated in the evening, when the professional standard shows were put on for a wide audience. Plays like 'Little Women' 'Bare Foot in Athens' 'Importance of Being Earnest'. We sang secular songs like the 'Country Garden' and 'Oh My Lover is a Fisherman'. On another day, we all tried to dress in as much green as possible. This was to observe the Arbor Day. Classes were held for half the day and the rest was Arbor. All the Malis (gardeners) were assembled, garlanded, thanked for the work they were doing, they were given presents. Our Principal did the 'Role Call' of trees that were on the campus. The Concert Chorus sang, 'I know a green cathedral,' and our soprano soloists with the most beautiful voice, sang Joyce Kilmer's, 'Trees.' "I think that I shall never see a poem lovely as a tree… only God can make a tree." Yes indeed only God can make the flowers grow, make all the racing rivers flow and turn the rippling water into solid snow.'

Later, each and every one, either individually, in pairs or in small groups planted saplings.

That's how we had our eucalyptus, guava and mango grove, green hedges and many other trees and plants all over the campus. This was a very beautiful day. Before the college was established the site lay barren. We all enjoyed looking around at the new creation.

With all the smooth sailing, one day was quite chaotic! That was the 'Servant's Day', when all of them were given half day off! And the girls took over, the Seniors were cooks and the kitchen their realm. The Juniors were in charge of laying nearly 200 places in the dining room.

The younger ones did not exactly know what they were doing. An air of chaos reigned! The food that day was, well!! at least edible!

The kitchen staff next morning found everything higgledy-piggledy! And far more utensils to wash and to bring the kitchen back to normality. After it all, peace was quite hilarious!

In my Freshman year. I had also started taking piano lessons. Much of my free time, if not roaming in the mango grove or the flower garden, was spent in the music room, at the instrument, a new but much-loved territory for me. My teacher always told me I was doing very well, but has that made me an accomplished pianist? Oh no, no, a mediocre one? Not even that. I still play the very elementary stuff. That keeps me well satisfied with myself. I always wanted to have a piano of my own, which now I have. When the piano arrived, it also had a label "Practice" on it. This was quite unfamiliar to me, and I did not like the looks of it. So, it was promptly shifted and left on a shelf, out of sight. With 'Practice' out of my way, I was at the liberty to play in my own creative way using the wrong notes as well. When I have done a lot and a lot of nothing. I am an expert at that! And my fingers feel frisky I tickle the ivories, good fun! Wrong notes do not matter. Why? They must be played, that's what they are there for. I must be the only one in all music realm, so highly capable of playing both, both the right and the wrong notes in the same basic piece. Even the concert pianist cannot do that. I can. I have my hat off to my exceeding excellence!

The Student Christian Movement, as expected was strong, and flourishing. They organised evening vespers held in the Chapel, and other Christian activities, including the beautiful Sunrise Services at Easter time, which were conveyed in the open. Another wonderful thing was the Annual SCM camp. Four from our college were elected to attend. I was glad to be there twice. It was a great blessing to meet others from different places, to share, learn and grow closer to knowing our Lord who so loves us.

General college life was kept happy and running well in order by the Student Government Association. No mishaps and no misdoing. The S.G.A are in charge of organising special dates like our beautiful Flowers Show, and had a big hand in the goings of the Sports Day. The SGA members were elected, and to confirm, there was a special inauguration service in the Chapel. I was glad, in my Freshman and Sophomore years to be elected the Hall of Residence floor proctor. Junior year the class representative and in the Senior year I was elected our Hall of Residence president.

The wonderful existence at college was fast waning and from all the games, singing and the moonlit skies, I got myself a Bachelor of Arts degree in Philosophy, English Literature and Geography. I wasn't quite done yet, so to add a bit more to myself, I stayed on to be a Licentiate of Teaching (now Bachelor of Education). A year of rigorous courses, lot of writing "lesson plans" and many hours of practice teaching-it was all worthwhile as at the end of it all, I came out a newly minted, sparkly, shining, full valued pedagogue, fully armoured, sturdy on my own two feet to face the Giant the open wide world

With all that, I still needed a strong support; I needed help; a sure unfailing help.

Whose?

Now and Evermore

I will lift up my eyes unto the hills, whence cometh help?
My help is from the Lord who made Heaven and Earth.
(Psalm 121)
"Lo, I am with you always"; "Ask and ye shall receive,"
Come unto me, all ye that labour and I will give you rest."

These are only few of the promises Jesus made to all of us and he surely keeps them.

The Lord is my shepherd. He keeps me and is my strong help. All my life seems to be His purpose and promises fulfilled in me.

The few incidences I write to prove His word never fails.

1. I was about eight, my older sisters were boarders. My eldest sister Catherine once became very ill. She had to be admitted to the hospital. Her illness became worse and the doctors started giving up hope of her recovery. She fell in a coma. A telegram was sent to my Dad asking him to come and see her. Dad left home and wherever he stayed, before going to see my sister, he as always prayed. During his prayer, he clearly heard a voice telling him, "Your daughter is

well." Straight away Dad went to see her. Sure enough, she was fine and opened her eyes and spoke to Dad. Catherine recovered and much to the doctor's astonishment, she was fully well and strong again.

2. It was round about at this time, maybe a few months later; We were having our lunch, when suddenly Dad heard a knock at the front door; none of the others of us heard anything. Before Dad could get up, John got out of his seat and said, "Dad, I'll go!" He came back to say that there was no one out there. After a few moments, the same thing happened. John came back again saying that there was no one anywhere near there. Dad said, "If I hear a knock again, we all will say 'Lord, speak, for Thy servant heareth.'" Surely, there was a knock again which only Dad heard. This time, he himself got up to see. He did not come back, so we all followed. There at the door was a petite, frail looking uncommonly attired Lady. Seeing her, someone like me would have sniggered, and be childish, but instead I could feel a calm come over me. We stood still, spellbound. I do not know what Dad said, as conversation with her was in English. When she left, Dad dropped himself on the sofa and uttered 'We've been visited.' Still the calm reigned over us. The question was who was she, and where had she come from, and then where had she gone? So frail and petite, she could not have gone far but on looking around, she was nowhere to be seen. Who was 'She?'

3. Our family had moved to another city. Our new house like most Indian houses had a flat roof, a meter and a

half high safety wall around it and of course, a wide staircase to go up there. This was a new found playground for me. I was just eleven but still frisky and full of climbing and jumping. The stairway made a good play for me. I loved running up and down it. One day, playing on the roof, a goofy goofy thought occurred, 'oh good, I'll get up on this wall and jump on the roof. What good fun!' When I got upon the wall and looked down to the ground, the ground looked so near. I was way up high on the top of the house and yet the ground looked so close. The more I looked down, the nearer the ground appeared and I thought "how wonderful, I'll jump down to the too close ground." All set ready to jump way down some thirty feet below, I crouched and moved; just then I felt a strong arm around my waist and instead of launching forward, I was planted erect firmly stable on the roof. I was extremely surprised and gasped (exact words) "Oh, what happened! Dad is not here!" I looked around, of course, Dad was not there, no one. I did not think much of it then, but what 'arm' was it that pulled me back? Now, I can only say, "He will not suffer thy foot to be moved." If He is not Omnipotent, if He is not Omnipresent, I would not be here today.

4. After that eventful summer holiday, I was a boarder at the Queen Victoria Girls High School. As I have previously said, I absolutely loved it there-I loved sleeping in the vast dormitory, with very high ceiling. In Summer, we all had to use our mosquito nets. To go to our washrooms, we went down a spiral

staircase, a couple of verandas and a covered corridor. Sometimes, we girls would leave our towel outside on the grass to dry to pick up later in the evening, or even the next morning. Once I left my bath towel like that with four others and did not take it back in the evening. That night we had a giant storm. Thunderous strong winds made windows and doors rattle furiously. Their sound made even me wake up. In an instance realising what was happening, sleepily I said, "Jesus my towel", and immediately fell asleep again. In the morning, there were effects of the storm everywhere; everything was covered with thick dust, blown up leaves and even with small twigs snapped from the trees. Storm had been devastating. Getting to my towel, I was stunned; it was a kind of a deep thud of amazement. It had a great impact on me. The furious storm had no power on my towel. It could not put a grain of sand or blown-up leaves on it and could not as much as even curl up the corners. The towel was just as I had left it. The other towels were victims of the storm; they were rolled up in sand and dry leaves and blown quite far! I was deeply struck. all I could say was, 'Thank you, Jesus.'

5. A year later, we were all at home for Christmas with usual festive air. We were also quite excited as our uncle, Dad's younger brother, whom he loved dearly was going to be married. Dad always wanted to bless the ceremony himself, but at this time, he was feeling really unwell with his diabetes. He desperately wanted to do the wedding himself. In his prayers, he heard a voice telling him that he will bless the

wedding. By the date of the ceremony, 27th December, Dad was well and strong enough to travel to and to solemnise his loved brother's wedding himself.

Two months later, our dear dad passed away. At this time, I was at school. We were orphaned at a very young age, yet all of us have done well in our lives.

Catherine, who once was very seriously ill and had survived against the doctor's word, ended with an M.A, M.Ed. from the Boston University and an MA, PhD from the Columbia University, New York, USA. She lived in New York. Emily was a Medical General Practitioner in Bradford.

John taught in a Methodist Public School in Truro, Cornwall. One year, he was selected by the English Speaking Union as an 'Exchange' to teach in Austin, Minnesota, USA. He was also a Counsellor for the Liberal Democrats, and was elected Mayor of Truro. This was our Queen's Jubilee year. When visiting Truro, John was her host. It was great seeing him on TV showing the Queen around the Cathedral. Later in the year, Her Majesty, as usual, for her garden party invited all her previous hosts. John was invited and I went along with him. What can I say? Yes, it was a beautiful evening and such a super experience to be in the Royal grounds.

My only brother was hugely talented. He had a super tenor voice and sang as a soloist in his choir. He was a keen photographer. His pictures were featured in several magazines. His paintings were displayed in exhibitions. But my most favourite of all was his ability to play any musical instrument just by ear. He revealed his talent from an early age. He did not know a note on the music score; he never had any music lesson. At the age of nine, he played the organ at the Cantonment Chapel Services, where Dad acted as an invited Chaplain. John played at weddings as well; how amazing is that!

In Truro, he was also a local Preacher. He spread the Gospel in many churches within his circuit.

I have a humble B.A, B.Ed. and much later added Dip SE.

Our youngest sister Mercy is very happily married in a very well-to-do Indian family. With an American citizenship, they live in Texas, USA. All these wonderful blessings to fulfil His promise – *"I will not leave you an orphan," "Lo, I am with you, always."*

I need His help in all my being and all my doings.

The Wide World

Fully equipped, I was quite prepared to dip my feet into the deep sea to get across to my post I've been assembled for. Now, I did not have a struggle making numerous applications; I had already been appointed at a school I was to teach at. The American Principal knew my Mum through the Church Conference, and had told her that I should teach at her school when I finish my training. So, there I was. I sent in my letter of acceptance at the All Girls Boarding Church School in Bengal – a few hours train journey from my Mum. The school term was to begin in June; after a lovely holiday in the hills I arrived at Asansol station. I was looking for a taxi but what perfect timing! There was the school bus that was waiting to collect a few teachers who had been on a group holiday. Now, I was already with my new friends. They warmly welcomed me. On the way, I felt I was dangling in the deep end as they were conversing in Bengali – all foreign to me.

Yes, I was stepping into totally new grounds with new language and new culture. To them, I too was a stranger; not speaking their language and not familiar with their ways. But strangeness was soon mitigated. I felt quite at home with such a friendly bunch. Bengali is the sweetest sounding language, I easily picked it up and was soon conversing with them.

The late Miss Irma D. Collins
Principal
Calcutta Girls' High School.
Played a great part in the early years of my teaching career.
(This picture was taken at her farewell from the school in Asansol, Bengal)

Arriving at the school, our Principal, Miss Collins, welcomed me warmly and was happy to see me. I was shown to my accommodations, and I well settled in.

Next morning was the first day of the new term. For assembly in the hall, the girls were in their places and the teachers in theirs. After hymn, prayers and other announcements, the Head introduced me as the new English teacher. At that moment, you could have heard a bomb of dumb silence and shock explode. The girls were stunned and looked as if they could not believe. The shock still prevailed. It was time to be in their classes. I was for the first time with my own set. The girls were lovely, polite and full of respect. Still they looked genuinely puzzled.

It so happened that the cause of all the shock and disbelief was soon revealed. I was the one underneath it all. The strange thing with me is, and I'm not complaining, actually I quit like and enjoy its effect. The 'little girl' who loved climbing trees and jumping around, was still lurking in me, and people saw 'her' more easily than me in my ripening years. When the girls first saw me they took me for a "new girl" and put me in a much younger class. When I sat with the teachers, they still thought I was someone just visiting their school. They were looking for a hulky school marmy new teacher, but she wasn't there. Instead, this twelve-year-old new girl was to be their senior most English teacher, and that surprise had caused the bomb to drop. I liked being with them; they were all very lovely and friendly girls. Having taken me for a twelve year old, outside the class hours, they even treated me like one, and eventually, my nick name was 'The little girl'! With deep respect and tender affection, they addressed me, 'The little Girl!' Then, it was a great good laugh! After addressing me 'you little girl', a bolder girl, came out with, 'you are strange in the classroom, we are scared of you like you were a lion, and here we are talking to you like you are a child!!

Did I love hearing that? bring it more!

As had happened before, this time I was the youngest teacher on the staff, and I absolutely loved being babied by everyone, especially by Miss Collins, our Principal. She was quite Mumsey towards me. She has played a great part in my life and I feel deeply grateful to her. Guess what? She even equipped me with a bicycle which I rode all over the school grounds in my free time. And, what more, I played Lexicon with her, too, in the evenings in her little cottage.

Teaching and working with these lovely girls was a good start to my career. The school atmosphere was very happy and pleasant. On Sundays, the Church service was enchanting. In the beginning, I could not understand the spoken word but the hymn singing, like the language, Bengali music is just as sweet. By and by, I could join in singing with the rest. After the service, back at school, the girls attended the Sunday School. First altogether then the teachers took their separate groups. I had mine too. It all was going very well. A little later, I was appointed the Sunday School Superintendent. The most I loved were the four best dates on the calendar. These were the Sunday School picnic, and a sports day when mostly informal games were played. It was good to see the girls having enjoyable time with running, sack race, potatoes and spoon, three-legged, flat races, and others. The third was the Christmas Pageant, and this would be the first time they were having a show in English. Everyone enjoyed it thoroughly. The fourth, the biggest, was the Sunday School Christmas Dinner for the girls and their parents who could come. With great help from people, it was good fun organising it. All went well and everyone had their fill and enjoyed.

I was having a wonderful time here in Asansol, gaining and strengthening my professional roots. The world was opening wider and I needed a change. I moved on and my next step took me to Kolkata. Here, I was now a member of a large number of teaching staff at the Methodist Calcutta Girls High School for a real large number of only day scholars. The school is known for its high standard of education and followed the English Curriculum preparing girls for what once used to be Junior and Senior Cambridge exams, and now for the GCSE (General Certificate of School Education). In the final year, many girls passed with distinctions and First Class. The school inculcated high aspirations for becoming Doctors, Lawyers, Accountants and so many did achieve their goals. It was great to have set my feet on a solid ground and a friendly and congenial group of people.

In the vast school building, with three sprawling floors, most of the classrooms were on the ground and first floors. All the pupils, and most of the teachers came from their homes; only seven or eight of us lived in. We had our dining room and a big lounge. Life was becoming rosier with lots of new experiences and wider fields to explore. Teaching such a large number was a challenge but not a big problem. It was a pleasure and privilege to be in the room with such polite and pleasant pupils.

Living in was fun too. Three of us had become close friends. Most of the outside things, we did together like going out shopping or just looking around the gaping city Kolkata. Both of my new pals had lived and were educated in England. One came from Brighton. She also had a trained super singing voice. The other had lived in London and graduated from the Royal Academy of Music as a concert pianist. She was also an Associate of the Royal College of Music. No wonder, I was so happy in their company. A greater fun was added when after dinner, in our lounge, on the Grand piano, the pianist would thrill us by playing some most beautiful music. Many times, she was called to broadcast her playing from the All India Radio. We would then listen to her on the air. My greater still, thrill was, when some four of us would play Scrabble, an offspring game of Lexicon. I was totally encaptured by it, and guess! who else was there? to play with us. Yes, my dear Miss Collins. She had been the principal at the Calcutta Girls School for several years, but, officiated in Asansol for some time. Miss Collins was a strong hand in the Bengal Conference. It was great to be within her gates again. How complete my joy was of being there!

Our school ground was adjacent with the Thorburn Methodist Church. Most of the girls came from Christian homes, but many were from other backgrounds; still with their parents' consent, all the girls were led into the Church for the morning service. It was great hearing them sing from the hymn book and seeing them being keenly attentive through the devotion.

On Sundays, I went to the church service and sang in the large full score choir. Our Anthems – works by great composers, sung accompanied with expertly played organ. The Women's Service Guild was held fortnightly I was their President. We met as a prayer group, with one of our aims to raise funds through various channels. The funds raised, were to aid, amongst others, our church medical work, and our Baby Fold, the Orphanage. This help was greatly appreciated.

Our Bishop had appointed me the Director of the Methodist Youth Fellowship. It was great meeting and visiting the young people in several different churches.

Sometimes, a train journey was made and an overnight stay at the vicarage. This was to enable me to address the whole congregation, to make them aware of the importance of their influence on the spiritual lives of the children amongst them. The Youth Fellowships managed and followed their own way but needed advice and encouragement and support.

The Church Minister also had a big responsibility in that.

All these wonderful opportunities were for my own enhancement as well, and I was immensely grateful.

I had also made connections with the Young Women's Christian Association. Outside school, and we had a lot of fun too.

One evening, my pianist friend and I randomly went to see a movie. The film was revealing the colour prejudice prevailing in England. To me, it was kind of an eye opener, and yet a disbelief. It turned out, the opening scenes were set at the Royal Academy of Music in London, where my friend had studied. She nearly called out loud, "My school, I have gone through those doors." How peculiar! Later, the scenes show the expansive Hampstead Heath. Seeing that the same sensation ran through me, as the one I had seeing the picture of the Royal Festival Hall a few years earlier. At that time, I had not the faintest notion that I'd ever see them myself someday.

During this time, my most beloved mum passed away; many were saddened who had received her deep kindness, her total selflessness and her vast generosity.

By now, my antennae were restless, my wings strong to spread and I needed to fly.

England

All this while, things were happening well and running smoothly. There was so much more to delve in to, like magic. But, it was no magic, and I know how, and much more was yet to come. The wide open world lay before me. From my childhood, I had a longing dream of travelling abroad, seeing places I would hear about, read and learn about in my lessons. It all was fascinating in theory; how wonderful it would be to see and experience these things myself. It was an impossible dream, and such things really happened only to others.

Now was the time for the doors to open for me and I was on the threshold of realising my dreams into reality. John and Emily were already in England. I had to get there. How?

Thinking about it planning began to take shape. First, I had to hand in my resignation from work at school, have a passport made, and make arrangements for my voyage. I had enough money saved up for the travel. The other essentials needed to be attended to. I went for my passport to the office, filled in necessary forms and was told the passport would be ready in a few days. That seen to, a very capable and reliable Travel Agents booked me on an Italian Boat 'Roma', that was to sail from Bombay to Genoa, a west coast port in Italy. The whole route from Bombay to London was impeccably organised; I just had to be on it. It was my last day at the school; I still did not have my passport. I was informed that it would be sent to their office and I could pick it up from there in Bombay. I felt a bit jittery but accepted their word. Now, I had to travel from one end of India in the East to the other in the West with miles and miles to cover in between.

A through journey in the train would have taken some six or seven days. India is vast. The liner was to depart on the 16th of April. I had to leave Calcutta on the first of April giving me ample time to cross the land to get to Bombay, one of the biggest cities in India. I wanted to give myself plenty of time to look around there but where would I stay? Suggestions were that I could easily stop at the YWCA being a member, or at the Methodist established Guest House. For some strange reason I chose the latter, and I was happily booked there. Now, my long journey started and I was all on my own with three large pieces of luggage and handbags in an Indian train! A young girl! Something not much heard of but I had no qualms, no fear of any sort. Actually, I was quite excited and cannot describe my feelings. After three long days from Calcutta in the train, I broke my journey in Lucknow, and stayed with my sister Catherine, for a few days. It was good visiting my college again and remembering all the wonderful times I had there. The games ground made me wish I could play there again, and the eucalyptus grove and the rose garden made me wish to linger on.

Time rattles on fast; the train was beckoning yet again. Still steely I boarded and after a lengthy long lapse of time made up of numerous, numberless hours, I had to land on completely new grounds all alone with three pieces of large and hand luggage. Thankfully, I had no mishaps.

Unbelievable things were still happening. Bombay, the station itself, a vast metropolis. In that, I had to find the coolie (a porter) who would carry my big load to a taxi who would take me to my destination. I still had no qualms in this almost a new country to me. A white bearded turbaned Sikh driver piled up my load on his taxi and we started off. Of course, I did not know where I was going and where he might take me; with no fear, I was confident. Sure enough, he brought me safely to the Guest House. What more and it was not thinkable and was unbelievable, when I opened my purse to pay him, after he had taken my things off the taxi, he with a twinkle in his eyes, a sweet smile and a sweet voice said, "O, leave it, leave it, you are my own little girl." How sweet and wonderful it was! He just wouldn't let me pay him, and he left.

There at the door was my very friendly, an American hostess waiting to receive me. I had a very warm welcome and was shown to my room-a most comfortable spot. I was settling in well, then later in the evening prepared to come down for dinner. A beautiful dining room and beautifully laid table; I was glad I had booked my days here at this Guest House. Here, a great amazement was in store for me. In the dining room we were shown to our seats and after Grace, we, new guests, in a good humour, were asked to introduce ourselves. As expected, I was totally new and did not know anyone there. When my turn came, I had barely finished saying my name that a bolt of shocking surprise!!

I was flabbergasted; a lady on the other side of the table called out, "O, you are Sarojini! How wonderful to meet you I am so pleased to see you." I really did not know what was happening; what it was all about. How could she have known me or even my name?

This lady was a resident here, and did some voluntary work with under privileged women helping them with literacy and numeracy. They also did some hand craft work with her. In India, we have our Methodist Church National newspaper circulated weekly. I had my poems included in two of the publications. Miss Childs had read them and liked them. One was 'The Upper Room' and the other 'Easter'. Now on actually seeing and meeting the author of the poems, she was happy. I too was very happy, also from being congratulated by all the others and having my poems appreciated. The conversation at the table was light hearted and jovial. I had an unexpectedly lovely evening, still trying to drink in the sweet kindness of the taxi driver and now Miss Childs reaction on seeing me. I wondered, if this was not why I mysteriously chose to come here!

But this still was not all the wonder and surprise. In the morning, after a good night's sleep, I came down for breakfast. When Miss Childs came in. She was holding something in her hands and had a huge smile on her face. She had brought in a little gift for me – a little souvenir made by her handcraft ladies. This was a small beautifully embroidered table cloth. I thought it was immensely kind of her and I dearly cherish having my gift. She said because she liked my poems so much and reads them from time to time that I should have this token to remind me of her appreciation.

I did not have much time in Mumbai and I wanted to look around as much as I could, but first I had to find my passport. Duly I arrived, there, a bombshell! Only to be told that my little book wasn't there. It was such a thud of a blow. Just as I turned to leave, a calm descended, a man came in with my passport. The blow blew away; I was thrilled.

My thrill was greater still when I saw the vast outreaching sea; soon I was to be floating on it. 16th of April, and that was the day I was to embark. My excitement was mounting higher, not ever having seen the sea nor the huge sailing boats, there, like a massive Palace mansion was anchored 'Roma.'

That was to be my home for the next few days.

The sixteenth of April was the time to embark.

My American hostess from the house and Miss Childs came to see me off. The travel agent's rep came to finalise the terms and to do all the essentials to see me boarded on the boat.

All my luggage was in the right place and I was shown to my cabin. The boat was ready to set off. We all came out on the deck to say our last Good Byes to the Indian coast. My two friends were still sweetly waiting and waving for me. Soon out of sight, we were well and really afloat on the vast expanse of water. Sadness, tears and fears were nowhere near me. I was floating with glee, having just checked in a vast luxury hotel for a long amazing holiday.

I had a lovely cabin, sharing with a friendly lady. My corner was spacious with a comfortable bed; for me it was a hard thought to take in. This huge hotel with vast halls, large dining rooms, well equipped library, sacredly set Chapel and even a large swimming pool was actually a floating boat. I was soon getting used to it. The sea was wonderful, a thrilling novelty for me. I found my favourite spot on the open deck and I'd stand there for hours staring at splashing, shining and shimmering waves dancing to the beat of the sun rays. Every wave created a new curve, ever changing, never the same, and no orchestra can match the chorus, the splashing of the water sang. How wrong the people, who warned me of the monotonous scene of the smooth water with nothing around for miles. The sea is ever changing and has a magic of its own. I was totally mesmerised; loved it immensely and felt I could never have enough of it.

Ever since coming to England had become a reality, I was thinking of the two completely new grounds I'd have to step into. The first one was going to be quite hard. Never as much as having to wash a teaspoon and having to step in a kitchen. I was always a 'sit and eat' and an outdoor girl. That aspect of living was going to be quite a challenge. How can it be that everyone does everything by themselves, I used to wonder. *Do in Rome as the Romans do.* I was quite looking forward to standing up to it all. The other was a mystery I had heard of but could not figure out what it was all about. I thickened my skin, should I really have to experience colour prejudice prevalent in England at that time. So far the English people I had known and had been friends with were charming, so warm, how could that phase be possible?

Most of the travellers in the boat were Italians; they were full of their humour and laughter. No place for me to feel 'foreign'. I liked being with my Italian friend, gorgeous blue eyes and perfect English accent.

The days with the waves were rolling fast. By now, I was a huge bag of joy and excitement.

We had sailed through the Red Sea and were on the Suez Canal, experiencing the so long heard of, the ingenious engineering of the 'locks', we entered the Mediterranean Sea. It all had been good fun, and a promise that we are getting closer and closer to our goal. At the other end of the sea. Arrived at Sicily, the boat anchored at Sicily harbour for a little while. We had ample time to come off and look around.

Just getting there!
A step off 'Roma' at Naples sea port.

Joe took me to see the vast Cathedral. What jaw dropping magnificence, and my first taste of touching European soil. It's a wonder I did not explode with all the excitement building up inside me. My qualms or any thought as to where I was, where I was going or what will happen next, were nowhere near me. I was quite easily and happily drinking it all in. We next were in Naples. Well and truly, Italy. We could step out and breathe the Italian air. At a distance the Vesuvius visible, still smoking. Soon the last lap of our voyage was over. We had arrived at Genoa where we were to alight, say goodbye to 'Roma', our floating hotel, good bye to my favourite spot on the Deck where I stood for hours watching the fuming frothing waves and the vastness of the proud sprawling ocean in its own peculiar glamour. From this moment on, things were, quite literally, happening mysteriously specially with my luggage. The last I had glanced on it, was when I set it off to be placed in the right place on the boat. Then next I saw it was in London, all in one piece, undented, undamaged. I myself have not the dimmest recollections of the transport and the transfers that had to be made; how we were fed or where we slept. I must have drowned in a long drowsy dream, that was soon to be evaporated.

From Genoa, we boarded a train traversing many countries to come to Calais in France. There, we boarded a ferry to cross the channel, and with a welcome from the white cliffs, we arrived in Dover. From the harbour, we boarded the Boat Train. Wow!!! At last actually in England!!!

Looking out through the window, it did not appear to be much different, excepting, I was quite puzzled seeing rows upon rows of terraced houses, built of bare brown bricks, low walled and such small doors!! Did people really live in them? I hadn't seen any one around. So, how do they get their pianos through those small doors? In my ignorance, I had believed that every home in England had a piano, and that everyone played it. I hadn't felt the spark yet, and the low walled brown bare brick built houses were still a bit of a shadow. In India, the roofs are much higher, and the buildings plastered and paint washed. By now, the accumulated excitement was dwindling, and a huge chunk of despondency was taking over, seeing the vast barren openness and the apparently abandoned, derelict structures. Yes, it was kind of a shock, and a much harder hit was yet to come. However I was still tightening up my ego to face the elusive prejudice.

Finally, we touched our ultimate destination. The train stopped, we alighted on the longed for grounds. My luggage, all in one spot, in one piece, was almost the very first to be loaded off. A porter, an English coolie, with a wide smile of a warm welcome, transferred my pieces to the check point. There again, I felt no qualms. The gentleman at the post, opened one of my cases, looked in, and must have asked me some questions, as to how I was, where I was going and so. I must have looked a bundle of pure innocence, he did not bother even to unlock my other two cases, and set me off.

Then, the bolt of a blow!! O, this is London?!! A disbelief in my sigh!! After Lucknow, Bombay and Calcutta railway stations, Victoria looked like a shack, with very low roof, and the dusty, bare brown bricks visible. The jolly porter took my luggage from the check point, where to receive me waiting were my two little nephews with my brother-in-law.

Emily's husband who was working for the BOAC, and that's how they were living in London. Emily, a Doctor was on duty, so could not come. I was wanting to see her, and could not wait. We got in a taxi and off! I was still in a deep shadow; the road looked so narrow and the traffic mainly, then in vogue, the bubble cars. Was I in Gulliver's Lilliput? So be it! I was quite excited I was in England, and with my family. Soon the shadows were melting away, as we were nearing the hospital where Emily was. What a delight!! and excitement on seeing her! My two little nephews were also with me who had come to receive me with their father. Now, all five of us were together after such a very long time.

Emily had her own room in the doctor's block and she had the guest room reserved for me where I was to stay. By now, I was feeling quite at home, having settled in my room and being with my family. This was Tuesday, the thirtieth of April and the marvels of London started opening up. I had stepped into this, so far, a land of dreams. The next day, which was the first of May, I saw the first morning and the first day light in England; it was a very beautiful morning and Emily's day off. She was taking me to show the true London. I was all excitedly geared for it. First my novel introduction to the underground. Yes I had heard of it but my puny brain could never comprehend how it really worked, trains running underground? Now, I was really going to be on one! Then the escalator, in itself a huge amazement for me, seeing a rolling staircase; I had loved running up and down staircases; this was a rolling one, so a much added thriller for me! I loved running down it with a childish glee. Then more wonder! A tiny toy train materialised and no engine! The doors opened magically. I was in another world of magic! The ride in it was enchanting. We arrived in the West End the Covent Garden, and wandered seeing the imposing Royal Opera House, famous Drury Lane. My eyes were bobbing out and the real splendour and grandeur of London was dawning on me.

We continued and walked down the North Bank of the Thames. First Cleopatra's Needle, how awesome the feat for it to have been floated down all the way from Egypt! Next was a thundery wallop! On the South Bank large and real stood the Royal Festival Hall, the building I had seen the picture of exactly ten years ago in the newspaper, and that had sent a strange sensation through me. Now I was seeing it in true life! I did not want to leave that spot; I stood and stared and stared at it. How I was feeling by now, my words cannot explain how I felt. Perhaps, I was dancing in the air.

The whole day had been most wonderful. I had started living on the pages of a super story book; I was enchanted by the Tube and thought it was one of the foremost amazing things London had. How can anyone get lost, and how easy it was to travel on. I was going to prove just that! The next day Emily was on duty so was my brother-in-law who would escort my nephews to a private nursery and set off to work. This would leave me at a loose end. What would I do? I knew what I had to do – go out and explore. The Tube was handy; a very good idea. I came out with the three of them and asked to be left at a salon as my hair needed dressing. First, I look some tips for directions of getting back. All agreed, all settled. I was now on my own. I had my hair dressed and felt very good with it. Leaving the salon. I started walking to where I'd be next, then I was a bit mystified seeing another Indian lady wearing a sari walking towards me. Am I seeing things? To make it stranger still, the lady's walk and the way she was attired strongly reminded me of my Professor at college. She taught me Geography some ten years before. How canny could it be? Yes, it was she, on meeting me she was just as surprised. We exchanged a few words. I told her it was my second day in England, and that I was staying with Emily, whom she also knew. My Professor had now become the Principal of our sister college The Women's Christian College in Madras. How wonderful that was! I was over the moon and wondered what Emily was going to say when I tell her that. I wasn't getting over it. After a little bit of more wandering around, and taking in the new sights, I arrived at the tube station to travel back to the hospital. First of all, I was quite excited with the news I had for Emily. I was sure she was not going to believe me. My train came and I found my seat. There were not many people in this car, but sitting apposite me was a kindly looking gentleman.

He came up, sat next to me and started talking with me. Somehow, he must have sensed I was new in London. I liked talking with him. He asked me my name – he could say it so easily, he asked how long I had been in England, and where I was staying. He told me his name, soon he was to get off, so wished me all the best, and assured me that I'd love London. Now understandably I could hardly contain myself. What will Emily make of it? Perhaps she will think I have lost my plot. Second day, let loose on my own in London. She did give me strange looks, but telling her more strongly convinced her. She did explode when I told her of speaking to a stranger, and who he was. She said, O it cannot be he, travelling in the Tube and talking to the likes of you. He is very famous, one of the top named gentleman. It cannot be he. So, how would I know his name, if he had not spoken to me. Finally, she accepted my story and with kind of a losers' voice said, "I've been in

England for so long and have never met any one important; your second day and you meet these unexpected people."

Second of May is my most memorable date. More and greater things were still in store for me. The process of my becoming a teacher in England was in the pipeline. I had filled in the necessary forms and all was going well from the authority. I only had to finalise my dates. It was middle of school term, so Emily suggested to wait till the new term, and go around and see more and more of London. This was music to my ears, as this is what I'd now love to do. With the travelling ropes finally in my hands, I felt free like a bird. I was feeling easy going around. People had been warm and friendly, and even literally going a second mile to help me, I asked a lady if I was on the right bus stop. No, she said and in spite of being laden with her two shopping bags, and instead of just pointing to where my stop was, came all the way to make sure. I was also deeply impressed by the way things happened in those days. There would be a pile of newspapers at the entrance of the underground, with no one in sight, just a large cloth left beside it. People would pick up their paper and leave the right amounts on the cloth. The money was not stolen, not even as much as shuffled. Similarly, shoes to be mended were left outside the cobbler's door, and the laundry at the launderers, what honesty! London to me had become a marvellous place. Unique!!

I was enchanted with people I had met so far were so warm, helpful and friendly. Where was this prejudice, I had prepared myself for. I was baffled, but needed to see it somewhere. I hadn't experienced it even in the slightest and I was hell bent on finding it, to have a taste of it myself. The only places I would see it quite strongly was on the advertising notice boards.

"Vacancy, no Blacks please, only Europeans need apply." This was a great puzzle to me and I just had to solve it. I am from India, not from Europe. Devilishly, I'd barge into big shops, thinking, this is where I'd be told, 'sorry this place is not for you and be turned away.' Oh no I'd still be met with that true English friendliness. "Hello, how are you, how can I help you." No I still did not find that prejudice. I had not been in England long and I was enjoying my freedom exploring and going around. I was still on the lookout for that 'P' this must have been my second or the third week when popping in and out of some shops, I spotted it. Eureka! I've found it! surely this is where I'll find it – that prejudice I'm after to see, I've heard of and seen on the notice boards. I spotted a Secretarial Employment Agency Office. Perfect grounds for fulfilling my quest. I am a teacher, no notion of even the 'S' of being an office secretary. Surely, this will be where I'll be turned away. I hardened my bones, and knocked on the door quite prepared to have it bang shut on my face. Gosh! My knees wobbled! It just was not happening. The door opened, and a very sweet kind lady welcomed me in. "Come in, do sit down." Deep within me, I was quite shocked with this gentle welcome. For a little while, she conversed with me amicably, then the question what are you looking for in the employment agency. I had to say I was looking for work. My scene had so unexpectedly and completely changed. I was in an offbeat. Office work not my plate. I was content with full belief, I'll be told this was the wrong place for me. The lady kindly asked me if I could type, I shook my head sheepishly and said 'no', she asked if I could do Short Hand and a second 'no.'

"So what will you do?" she asked.

Timidly, I said, "O, anything." My heart now firmly believing I'll be told there was nothing for me there, and that I could not be helped. My being so new in London could also be a great block. But what a gigantic surprise and thunderous pleasant shock.

After several phone calls here and there, she had actually found me a job. I had a job in an office! What I had come here for, and instead what did I get! My heart crinkled. I was given a place at the Income Tax Office in the centre of London in its busy part, off the famous Regent Street. My world completely turned upside down. I, a teacher, new in London, had no intention, even in my wildest dream to do anything else but teach when the time came for it. Now, with no applications, no interviews, I was in London, an employee in an entirely new field. I was delighted, yet bolt struck with what had just happened. And, what will Emily say to this? Perhaps, that I really have gone bonkers.

She had left me to explore and familiarise myself in the new spots I'd venture into. Instead, I'd landed myself in a job. It did take quite some convincing her, but at least she liked my story. On Monday, the second June, smartly dressed, I arrived at my office, the Income Tax one. I was well received, and was shown my desk I was to work at. Many people working, no shorthand, no typewriters in view. Everyone busy with their paper work. I had to start at the very simplest task of checking mail and some filing. All very easy and felt more like good fun than a load of work. I soon took to it, and it was wonderful meeting so many friendly people and seeing a different scene of the world, where other wheels turn.

My sister also had a flat in Crouch End. It made it easier to get to the office from there than coming all the way from the guest room at the hospital. I was quite enjoying my new work, also an eye opener to see how the other half of the world lives.

At this time, I also joined the Young Women' Christian Association, I already was a member of in India. It was to be singing again, I was in the choir. Our director was young, bubbly and full of life. I loved her piano playing. We learnt and sang many great works, among them Bellini and Puccini's Masses, the various 'Requiems', and I absolutely loved singing the chorus parts in the Gilbert and Sullivan's Trial by Jury and the Mikado. Our choir met every Wednesday evening, and it was just one stop on the tube to get there from the office. From the YWCA I'd walk to the underground. At the other end of the tube travel, I'd take a bus to drop me at a stop, a short distance from the flat where I was staying.

I had become quite used to using tubes and buses I needed for travelling. It was all convenient and safe. At a bus stop, if a bus was delayed or there was a wait someone would start to converse. Not deep yet more often, it would be just have you been waiting long? Or how far do you live? Just an informal chat not quite pin pointing exactly where one lived.

I was quite enjoying the fun at my work and what more! I was getting my own money! Things were happening wonderfully well with me. Time seemed to be moving fast; weeks and months rolled happily. Soon, it would be Autumn and then Winter. I was so looking forward to seeing the snowfall; also to experience thick fog I had heard of. The days started becoming shorter, and the air a bit colder. In a few weeks' time, the evening was much darker and the air a lot colder. We would also hear of fogs occurring here and there. People were still using log fires for heating, and the smoke was causing the fog. Traffic on the roads was affected. There were car accidents and buses were halted because of poor visibility. I still hadn't seen the fog happening but I was soon to experience it.

One Wednesday evening, it was quite dark. As usual, after the choir, I walked from the YWCA to the underground. At that other end I got off to get to my bus stop; by the time I got there, fog had drifted in. In minutes, it was extremely dense, let alone the right hand not able to see the left hand, I am sure my thumb could not see my first finger. There was no one else at the stop; I had arrived there all alone. In the distance, they announced 'no buses.' The visibility was absolutely nil. In that pitch darkness, I could not see or even sense anyone near there. Yet in that deep density, I heard a voice that said, "You need the bus? O, I'm going that way come with me." I still could not see anyone not even faintly. But no questions asked as to how and how far; I just followed the Voice. I could not even see the ground I was walking on; I just followed. The Voice was not walking beside me but a few steps ahead. With no questions, qualms, hesitation, I was following the Voice. I was then warned of a stone I was coming to, warned of the kerb I had to step up to. Then, still the most amazing, the Voice said, "O, I know a shortcut, I'll take you." Again no question asked, no doubts. I did not know where I was walking I just followed that Voice, and in no time, I was at my flat. My real travel would have taken much longer. In that pitch darkness. I had followed a strange Voice, and I was at my flat all safe and so well guided. Who was that Voice? Who knew the way, even a shortcut and led me to my house in that solid dense fog. How did they know exactly where I lived? I did not stop even to say a Thank you. I was safe inside. It was much later when I thought of that mystical experience, and remembered the two men who had walked with an unknown Stranger but later realised who He was. I, then realised it was that same Stranger who had walked with me and made my steps so sure footed. How amazing, how great, how wonderful, I thank you, my Lord, my Keeper!

Now, I had experienced the fog; time to see the snow was soon coming. Well, it did and I was like a child! At the office, I saw a few tiny flakes fall, I jumped off my seat, ran to the window and called out, "O look, look the snow!" As if the others had never seen it. I caught a few flakes in my hand and went round showing everyone. "Hey look! Snow." I was immensely excited seeing the snowfall. This meant, it was December, the year was to be ending. By now, my sister had enrolled herself in Dublin, where she would study further to fulfil her aspiration of becoming a Medical General Practitioner. She would be leaving London and I'd have to find my own digs. There was still quite some time and I had to start looking around. Oh, where would I turn? Things had been happening wonderfully well with me. I had already had my holiday from the office; I had just a few more weeks to complete my time there. My teaching appointment was finalised. I was to start in January, just after finishing work at the Income Tax. Search for my digs had not begun, I'd soon get going on that.

One occasion just before the choir I went into the cafe. There at a table a lady beckoned me. I did not know her. She was not in the choir. We introduced ourselves to each other.

She was from Mauritius and was on holiday here in London like several other times before. She had mostly rented a room in the house where she was staying now. She knew London well and had made some good friends. Her work was with the young Christian people, similar to what I had done in India through my church. I told her about myself, how long I had been in England, what I was doing and that I was living with my sister who would soon be leaving, and I'll have to find my own place. To that, her immediate response was, "O, you'll find a room at the house where I am. I'll tell my Land Lady and she'll accommodate you." There I was! I did not have to go house hunting; I had found one!

Emily was extremely pleased and was relieved that when she leaves, I would be safe. At the house, the Welsh Land Lady welcomed me warmly. I found her to be quite Mumsy! I was happy having to step into a new sphere but was nervous with the thought that I would now be completely on my own two feet. To begin with, I needn't have worried. My room was next to this new friend who was very helpful and showed me the initial ropes.

She took me to the shops and helped me with buying and getting me acquainted with the essential pots and pans and basic groceries, tea, salt, bread, butter, cereal. It was good being next to her. She even shared her breakfast with me and I still did not have to put my hand in a cooking pot yet. I'd have to do all that myself very soon, though. My friend's time in England was coming to an end. Just before leaving, she introduced me to two of her friends who were not far from me. An English lady, the other Swedish who was supervising a hostel for working girls from Sweden. Both my new acquaintances were most amicable and offered their help should I ever have a problem.

At the house, I was now on my own, and my utterly new life well and truly started. I was, for a bliss, in a comfortable and friendly place.

My next-door neighbour helped me come to terms with the cooker. It took a lot of mishaps and quite some time to get over that hurdle, and I could make tea and breakfast myself. This was English life!! Time was rolling fast. My term at the office was closing. I was to stop at the beginning of January. Everyone there came to say Goodbye. I was given a large box of chocolates and a huge bouquet of blooms. I was sad leaving there, but eagerly looked forward to getting my hands into the work I was prepared for.

It was Monday, the fourteenth of January, when I had to begin at a secondary all-girls school in the East End. Being a starter in London, I was a 'Supply Teacher'. What was strange! I felt I was back at the Calcutta Girls High School! Here the girls also wore the same uniform – white blouse and denim skirts. What, still more! The music teacher, an American had lived in Calcutta and had attended the same church as I had, a little before I was there. Still, we had something in common and could exchange notes. All this made me feel 'how small the world was!' I liked it there, as the girls were respectful and attentive. I liked it there as three others on the staff had become very good friends, and they did not live far from where I was, so we travelled back home together. I had quite a bit of a distance to the Tube, then I caught a bus to get to school. I found this too tedious and rushy in the early morning. Before the summer holidays, my friend suggested, it would be good if I found somewhere more convenient. This was a good idea. I had already booked my holiday abroad, My friend said, when I get back, she'd help me find a new place. She also kindly offered to keep my things with her until then, thereby I could give up my room at the Welsh house, and save my week's rent. This was extremely thoughtful of her. I felt very sad leaving there as I was very warmly taken care of.

My vacation in Switzerland was amazingly wonderful. When I returned from there, a shock! My friend had not yet got back. Ah! What was I now to do? Where do I go? A bright idea! I thought of my Swedish friend, not far from me, I could tell her my story. So, sweetly she came to my rescue, and made me feel at home in a vacant room at the hostel. I could stay there until I needed. There were still some days for the new school term to start, that gave me time to look around for my own lodging. I had seen the snowfall and had experienced the thick dense fog, but I still hadn't come anywhere near the slogan for 'Europeans only!'

Now was the best chance for me to get a taste of that also. Notice boards in the shop windows were full of "no blacks need apply" or, "For Europeans only", "no blacks please!" Not just notices, but I had also heard of incidences of non-welcome, I thought surely this was my ground to know what it really, actually means. Hell bent on easing my quest, I tightened my nerves and stiffened my legs seeing an old advert for a vacant room, with the same slogan, for "Europeans only, no black please". This was my target I wore my steely armour fully prepared to have the door bang shut on my face, I knocked, and was completely shattered with the response. I was shaken. A kindly lady opened the door and in such a smiling way, she asked what she could do for me. This was not at all what I had expected; this was not what I had prepared myself for. How could I even have imagined that I'd find an accommodation in this house. Of course, there was no vacancy there. Then, with her smiling gentleness I was crumpled within. A bigger bomb was yet to drop. As I turned to walk away, she called me back to say that within a few days, a room will be available and I'd be very welcome to stay there, What? What? I felt crushed with what had just happened.

I was out with my prank expecting a completely opposite outcome. Anyway, to my tremendous shock, surprise and enormous thrill, I was offered a room at this house which was advertised, "For Europeans only." My Swedish friend was very pleased that I had found an accommodation. When my English friend got back, she too was very pleasantly surprised that I had already found my new lodgings. She transferred my luggage there, and helped me settle in a house, "for Europeans only"! For me, it was like walking into a new haven, everything proved to be perfect. It was under five minutes to the bus and the tube station, with all the other amenities within easy reach. My room was comfortable with constant hot water, bed linen and regular servicing provided. The caretaker lady who had welcomed me was amicable and helpful. I made some good friends there and lived at that address for many and very happy long years.

So where was that prejudice? I hadn't found it anywhere and it is most wonderful not to see those notices anywhere anymore. England is such a warm friendly place. Everyone is welcome, all colours, class and Creeds live together in perfect harmony, making England truly Great.

Teaching and Retirement

I think teaching is the best profession. Everyone in the world who has had a chance, had the privilege of having a teacher to build and construct their individuality. All the Prime Ministers, Lawyers, Doctors, Scientists and all the other professions have relied on their teachers. To be a teacher in itself is a great privilege and I'm grateful to have had that opportunity.

Here in England, being new on the role, I was a Supply Teacher. I did not know what it meant, but through experience I learned I was to fill in for an occasional absent teacher. I started at a Secondary all-Girls School and taught there for a whole year. I "Supplied" for long terms at various other schools. I enjoyed doing that as it made me see different set ups and locations. But my true commission was soon to be revealed. I was called to fill in for a few days at a Partially Hearing Unit, at a Junior School. This would be an entirely new ground for me to step into.

My training and long-time experience was in the Secondary Sections. To add to this, to deal with this disability would be totally novel. Seeing so many young children with this imparity was heart rending. Not only did they have to struggle with their shoe laces and shirt buttons but also the added cumbersome hearing aids and the batteries around their waists. I tried soon to soak in the situation, and dealt with it as best as I could. Then, I was very happy when I was asked to stay on till the end of the term in spite of the return of the teacher I was filling in for. The experience was a new stage of learning and for my own development. I consider the loss of hearing as one of the hardest inabilities to cope with. I was learning the aches of having to live with this imparity. My quest was finding ways to be a real help in the lives of these innocent children. This was a happy place and the children eager to learn. The big plus for me was that my Head was pleased with me and satisfied with what I was doing. I contentedly stayed there till the end.

After the week's half-term holiday, being still a Supply, I'd be asked to fill in at some other school. But how wonders happen! One day during this gap, I was at a tube station on a crowded platform waiting for my train. The train arrived, doors opened, the crowd jostled to get in, just then I heard my name called from inside the train. I was a bit startled, but this was the 'Head' from the Partially Hearing Unit. There was an empty seat next to her. I sat with her, she sounded very pleased seeing me, with the usual "how are you and where are you going?" She asked me what I was doing after the holidays. Of course, I did not know where I'd be placed, so how I did I feel when she asked me to come back to the unit. "O, the children liked you and they will be happy having you back." I most gladly accepted. I was thrilled and thankful that there would be no waiting or curious suspense as to where I'd be in the new term. I was all fixed, and looked forward to being with those lovely children again. But how very strange for all this to happen! For me to be standing in the large crowd just at the right spot, for the train doors to open just in front of me, for the Head to be in that train and to be on the side from where she could see me. For the seat just beside hers to be empty. What caused it all? miracle?

After few more days, I happily went back and was lovingly received by the dear little ones. The 'Unit', a part of a regular Junior School was not very big. I had a few children of six or seven of age in my class. They were delightful kids learning in the normal way, but with the hearing loss, their speech was affected. It was my added intent to help them with their speaking as much as possible. I had to find my own ways for this to happen. Children of this age can have other hinderances also. In some cases, extra input was needed to get good effects. I had to work tricks up my sleeves. I still laugh remembering what I cooked up for this little one. He was bright, was learning to read fluently, with almost perfect speech, yet, he seemed to have a mighty dread of writing. He just would not do it. I had to get him out of this lock. Well, in his writing time, we played marbles. The more we played, the more he laughed. We had only two marbles-one for him and one for me. I wanted some more marbles for myself, so I drew marbles. Now, he wanted more marbles too. What does he do? He picked up a pencil and drew some marbles on his book for himself. He wanted to have more than I had. He wanted beautiful coloured ones. Soon, the marbles became letters. The beauty of the Roman script! Each letter of the alphabet being a marble or a straight line. His letters soon became words and words made sentences. He was now doing his writing happily. I was pleased to have achieved my goal seeing him smiling.

I have another anecdote I treasure most dearly in all my teaching years. This was a doll of a little girl, bright blue eyes, and flowing blonde hair. She had never spoken nor did much of anything. From her younger days, she was labelled as Autistic, with a question mark. Her grandmother used to bring her to school, sometimes crying, 'She's my eldest grandchild, and I have never heard her speak.' This to me was extremely touching, and literally pained me seeing her this way. The little girl, when called or spoken to only responded with her eyes and looked. In the class she would curl herself up and just sit. She was my charge, I had to find ways of making something of her. I had to devise most gravely unusual channels to help her. I was glad. When by and by there was an effect. From her 'curl', she started becoming active. It was also very good to see and realise that her hearing was not too impaired; she started to talk well and audibly. I was pleased, having her like others. Now, one day, when her grandmother came, she was bursting with delight, all beaming and saying, "Once I had never heard her speak, now my eldest grand child does not stop talking and cannot sit still!" How wonderful to hear that was! The very next day, the 'little girl' did not come to school, which had not happened before. Two days later, when she came I asked her the reason for her absence. She said that her grandmother had died. Had she waited all this long, just to hear her granddaughter speak? This was very hard to take in, I felt sad for the 'little girl'!

The years were passing. I was glad to have found my vocation here. I myself had learnt much and count these years to be my best rewarded ones. From the 'Unit' the children were passed on to higher school. The 'little girl' also left. I had come here as a Supply but stayed for a few more years.

In this time, I was also put on the Permanent Role, even without a required visit from a Senior Inspector. The 'Unit' was shrinking and, thankfully, there were not many more new admissions.

After this time, I was transferred to another all age Special Needs school. This school, initially for Delicate Children, Children needing medical attention during the day, but was now open for all; the 'Referral' case children who were not able to cope with normal education for some reasons or another. This school was not far from my house and much easier to get to. But, my episode of the 'little girl' who was now at a secondary school has not entirely ended. One day just out of the blue, I wanted to go to visit the Unit to see what had remained of it. Or what was happening there. I arrived to see that in only one classroom, there were a few kids who, when they finish at the last time, the 'Unit' was to close. The children were pleased to see me again, just as I was happy seeing them all grown up. But how mystically amazing!! That very day who else was there? The 'little girl' not realising what changes might have happened at the Unit since she left, she had come specially to see me. What extreme coincidence for me to go there that day, and for her also to have turned up!! Then, I nearly had tears in my eyes. Not had she just come to see me, but also had a little present for me. How sweet is that! I just do not have words to express how I felt then. Those moments are my most dearly cherished memory. And the largest cherry on the cake of my teaching career. I wonder if this moment was not the reason why I stood on that very spot on the crowded platform of the underground.

During the years after renting my abode for so long, I was able to buy my own. Just two short bus stops from where I lived, so far, was a prestigious block of flats. I found my little studio there. It was large enough for me. The young gentleman I bought it from, generously included all the furnishing and furniture in the price. All I had to do was move in. I was very excited also, because this was the very first time in all my life, I was to have my very own place that belonged to me. The block was beautifully maintained and its location made it more convenient to travel. I even laughed with my brother, who lived in Truro, Cornwall, look I just have to go through a long corridor to come to you. I was well connected with wherever I wanted to go. My flat on the second floor had a fair view of the far distance. In the west, I could see the hill with a church perched up on the top, and thought how marvellous it must be around there. This is Harrow where the famous school stands. What makes it more poignant, is that the Indian Prime Minister Jawaharlal Nehru, and the English Prime Minister, Sir Winston Churchill had both studied there.

All was going very well with me. The new school, I was now at, was a short distance from me, and the bus stop being almost at the door step, made it very easy to get to. Initially for the Delicate Children the school catered for any special educational need, another challenging ground for me.

Now another door opened for me, I enrolled myself at the University of North London, for a two-year evening course. The Thesis, Role of Computers in Education. Computing is a strong medium for building self-confidence in children and for enhancing their curious inventiveness. At the end, I was glad to have added a Dip Se, after my name together with the already B.A; B.Ed.

Having thrown in my lot at regular teaching for so many years, I took an early retirement. Not to give up completely, I was a 'Supply' again. Going to several schools was an excellent experience working with the different stages of learning.

With the freedom of having my own time, the decision was to revisit India. I booked to spend a month there. This would give me ample time to see some of my family and to go to places I knew. To begin, I was to stay with my cousin in Delhi. Her husband was the Secretary General of the Young Men's Christian Association there. He had been to the UK, also in connection with his work. I had to fly from Heathrow, but it was not a direct flight. I had to change planes. On rechecking in, my given seat was by the window and I waited for the other two seats to be taken. That did not happen, and I felt quite lordly having the pew to myself. What made it more exceptional and amazing was, that in the middle section of the plane was a jovial group of young people. They were also going to spend some time in Delhi having been invited by the YMCA. They all knew my cousin and had met him personally on his visit in the UK. They were very happy to meet me so unexpectedly and were excited to show me photographs taken with him. All this incidence made my flight to India a very pleasant one. On arrival at Delhi, the group was husked away in the YMCA bus, and I was taken home. It was good to be with the family and the new young ones I had not seen before. India had changed so much from when I left there. I gasped almost in shock to see so many people everywhere. Far more cars on the roads and the pavements pressured with pedestrians. With all this, I managed to travel and visit places of my gone by days. Being there again was a great fascination, yet a mingling of tinges of sadness. The great alteration made me feel I was in an entirely new country.

A few years earlier, the Theological Seminary had closed down. Three imposing buildings were being used for other purposes. The Kindergarten had turned to housing. The tree I loved climbing, in spite of my Dad's dread, was still there. Oh, did I want to climb it again, and put a swing on it! The memory was too deep and I did not move from there, I just did not, want to! The house where I lived was someone else's now. O, how was it possible?

I had the similar strong emotional feelings everywhere I revisited. In Lucknow, the Isabella Thorburn College just as great and glorious, now with many more students scurrying through the corridors. The Volleyball, Basketball and the games ground just the same. The distant Eucalyptus grove with its silver cylinder trunks and twigs where I romanced with the moonlit skies, was just as enticing and the glamour of the garden of roses just as alluring. How could I have ever left there?

I was itching and could not wait to go to Agra, extremely excited to see the amazingly amazing Taj Mahal in its enchanting magnificence. There I wanted to be the school girl again, picnicking on the cherished ground. I had seen this white marvel of marble several times before, on school trips and with the family. This once was yet another one. Taj Mahal, the highest, deepest and unique expression of intense love, will never cease its awe and wonder, but, what is that to me? I was much more strongly pulled by what had been my earthly paradise, my perfectly perfect haven, the Queen Victoria Girls High School. Every Brick seemed to cast the same spell on me I had felt, as a boarder, all through my growing years, I still could not tell what had made it so enchanting, so magical for me. I had just so, so loved that place.

The set up, now was enormously changed. With a separate new building for the boarders. The dormitory on the upper floor where I loved sleeping lay ghostly bare. Our washrooms converted to Science laboratories, as the school has vastly expanded to become an Inter college. For that, housing the classrooms for the higher education, a huge structured block now stands in the once empty space beyond the east garden and the tennis court. What had been the dining hall had turned into a Nursery School. In spite of these vast changes, I could still see myself in those fairyland days. I did not want to leave, they literally had to pluck me away. It was hard to leave from there.

Next on my list for a revisit was Calcutta. Again, a bag of nostalgia! And, as time changes, here was no exception. It was a delight seeing IRMA Collins Memorial Hall, newly built on the Girls School campus, named after the previous principal; yes, the same Miss Collins who had played Lexicon and Scrabble with me. She was much loved for her great services to the school and to the church. The hall was beautifully furnished for various school purposes.

A short travel took me to the place where my mum was the doctor. It was not surprising, yet, deeply touching to have so many people coming to see me. With affection and gratitude, for the medical work my Mum had done there.

My next sojourn was to be in Madras (Chennai); this was going to be quite an adventure. I had covered the full continent from east to west, and places in between. I had never gone South, now was my time for doing just that. It was a long journey, but I was glad to have made it. Being so much near the equator the peninsula is much different from the North. It was most interesting to see miles and miles of tea plantations. I was mesmerised on a day's visit to a Crocodile Sanctuary. These colossal lizards lying around, not a care in the world! Basking and soaking the sun.

I thought Chennai was an amazing place. I was spellbound seeing the tremendously huge ancient temple, covered with carvings of unrecognisable human and animal figures, way, way up in the sky. What mind blowing patience and intense diligence in creating such exuberance just by using simple primitive instruments and ancient expertise! I liked South India with its rolling hills and novel flora. It also brought the culmination of my travels; in the land I knew, from the tree tops and had roamed in under the moonlit skies. My feet turned back once more to dear London, my home.

Happy again, it was views from my studio windows and buses running from the door step. A month's adventure in the past was a lost dream, and life moulded to its usual. I was still a Supply and enjoying going to schools I had been specially asked for several times, and some quite new to me. 'Time waits for no one', and I seemed to be piling up years by leaps and bounds, I could not feel any difference, but my studio started to become smaller; I needed to spread myself in a house all of my own, with wide open spaces to surround me. A quiet uninterrupted spot would do well in my ripening years. Perhaps too much to wish for in London. The block where I lived was on a very busy road, and the nearby places too built up. Where was I to look, where would I find open spaces and the quiet and calm? My brother sent me leaflets, suggesting I should live somewhere south out of London. Was I to consider that? At that point, my greed burst out; transport in London is free, and my heart yelled, 'stay in London I love it here.' Instantly, I flicked the leaflets and commanded (exact words) 'Jesus, over to you, you find me a house and look in it I want' – a list of I want followed. Immediately, my hands were washed off having to look around, and even of wondering as to where I might live in this vast city of London.

In a day or two, I was 'Supplying' at a school in an area new to me. Coming back from there, to get to the tube, I came across an Estate Agent. They let me have a few brochures to look through. As I was scanning them, I saw a house for sale and well within the reach of my puny purse. Of course, that house soon belonged to me. What was so exceptional, it was located in the same area I used to view from my window and thought, how marvellous it must be around there.

The house fulfils all the 'I wants' I had asked for, open spaces, back and front peaceful and so quiet. I laughed with my friends; "you could hear a pin drop even on the grass!" I have wonderful friendly neighbours and transport being so near, shopping is convenient; I breathe in big airy rooms. I am fully convinced this house was specially 'found' for me. Seeing that even my name was already written on it! At the back in a good-sized garden is a pond. It had gold fish and pots of flowering; Sarojini, my name is a Sanskrit word for lotus blossoms. Lotus is also the Indian national flower. Now those distant hills with the church perched on top are just a stone's throw from me and I have visited that famed school with my friends. I am very happy and comfortable in my house and love sitting in my conservatory I had had built a year after I moved in. It is beautiful watching birds coming to peck in the garden to rest and to drink water from the pond. I also have an apple tree and a loquat tree I grew from seed; it being tropical, I did not expect it even to last, but it has grown wide with heavy foliage. It never sheds it deep green leaves, not even in winter, just here and there, soon to be renewed. Both the trees have given me ripe fruits in season.

I myself, in spite of the years have kept excellent health. I still do not need specs and have not touched a walking stick. I was a bit surprised when one day in my shower, I felt a tiny lump on my right side. I took no notice of it. Day by day, the lump was growing bigger, still no heed from me, until it started becoming very painful too. My stubbornness gave way. I went to see my doctor, she had barely touched me, and said, I should have gone to see her earlier. She immediately made an appointment for me for an X-ray at the main hospital. Very soon the fixed appointment letter arrived from the hospital. I had to be there the very next day. Clutching this note, I commanded (exact words) Jesus, 'do not let this happen to me, do not let this happen to me.' On the day, later to go to report at the hospital, as usual I went in my shower. I was surprised, I felt no pain at all, and the big lump almost the size of a golf ball was not there. No pain, no lump; I was my whole self again. All I uttered was, 'Thank you, Jesus.' He whose hands could wipe away leprosy and whose voice alone could raise the dead, what was my pain, what was my lump for Him? I had to keep my appointment. A half hour travel to the location. There, a doctor came to check me previous to the X-ray. She poked and prodded but her face was saying, "what are you doing here? There's nothing there." For a double check, another doctor came to see me. She also gave the same impression, I still had to have the X-ray. The nurse who took it came out with a big smile. "You are ok; your X-ray is all clear."

I have had no lumps or pain since then. I only feel truly grateful to Him who keeps me. After moving into this house, I still kept on doing 'Supply' and several other things I had been involved in. As the years have rolled on, I have stopped and take it easy. I make no plans for the day and move where the Fancy tells me to. All my doings are erratic; I like it that way; time and dates do not exist for me. Sometimes, morning comes too early. I do not take any notice and sometimes, the night is too late to begin. Leisurely and slowly, I have drifted to the verge of that great River I yet have to cross. That will happen only, when on the other side, my mansion is fully prepared, with the minutest detail, in that Great House. And, I shall be safely carried there in the Arms of my Keeper, my Shepherd.

Choirs and Clubs

I have always loved singing, and Sunday School days were the firm foundation for that. I'd be singing whenever and wherever, as loudly as I could. Mostly sung, were the choruses, "Give me oil in my lamp", "This little light of mine", and my most favourite, "Jesus loves me", and the nursery rhymes, "Baa Baa black sheep" and the best one, "Jack and Jill". Singing expanded in schools at morning prayer assemblies with hymns, or in small groups for Scripture shows. Actual choir started at College. Great works and Anthems, to sing at our main City Central Methodist Church services. In Calcutta also, I sang in our church choir. In London, choir horizons widened and more opportunities opened to sing with several different groups. Almost as soon as I came to London, I joined the Y.W.C.A. choir. It was great fun meeting and singing with lovely people in a new environment. I enjoyed learning new works. Not long after, another huge group of a thousand voices was enmassed. Voices from various choirs. We were to perform, in its entirety, the Handel's "Messiah". This was to be sung at the vast hall of the Alexandra Palace, to raise funds to overhaul the run down organ there. The whole project was constructed and conveyed by the eminent Maestro Violinist and

Conductor, Sir Yehudi Menuhin. He was passionate, and deeply wanted to have the organ restored. As for me, it was an amazing experience, singing with a large number, to a packed hall of listeners. What was my great sensation above all, was meeting and actually speaking with my school day icon. What a Great Man! Superbly gentle and a pillar of humility. Our singing went off well, and it all had to be done again the following year. For me! A repeated excitement.

At the YWCA, we continued singing some great works, with our young and highly talented music director. I especially liked her style and intonation of playing the piano. We had just started on Verdi's Requiem, when over the weekend, our young director and one of the choir members went to Scotland for a music seminar. In their off time, when possible, they were looking around, taking photographs and so. With her camera and looking for an apt spot, the pianist stepped too for back over the edge of the hill. The result was too tragic. A dreadful shock to her companion and thunderous blow and sadness for all of us. We further rehearsed the Requiem and sang at a special service in her memory and honour.

I moved on and joined the Westminster Choral Society. Another new venue, environment and a brilliant director. More great works and thrill of singing at some lovely venues such as St Martins-in-the-field and St James, Piccadilly. In time other doors opened. Though not a member, I sang with the London Chorale, a prestigious group. I felt deeply privileged singing with them at Opera Gala concerts to packed audiences at some outstanding venues, such as Fair Field Hall in Croydon, the Barbican, the Royal Festival Hall and the Royal Albert Hall. Similarly, it was great being with the

Barclay's Bank Musical Society, performing works by the leaders of musical renaissance in England in the nineteenth century, Sir CV Stanford and Parry. These were sung at the Great Southwark Cathedral.

My greatest ever joy, deepest sentiment came from Elgar's, 'Dream of Gerontius,' which was rendered at the exclusive St Paul's Cathedral. Even being at the rehearsals reminded me of my very first visit there with my brother, a few years earlier. It was quite an enchanting feeling just being there, we had a good look around the grounds, and inside I was excited going up the dome. Only to hear about the, Whispering Gallery was a great surprise, I just had to try it. My! What a marvel! Every word whispered got around that dome. Stepping outside on that height was yet another marvel. On that clear day, the views over London were breath-taking. I was reliving the experience of that day, but much more vividly, I was reminded of the moment when, I was quite small at home, our Dad was reading his newspaper and strangely, he called all of us. I popped up on his lap and he, in his solemn tone showed us the picture of St Paul's Cathedral. The war bomb had flattened most of the buildings around it But it escaped any damage. Dad said a prayer of thanks and assured us of God's greatness. Now, here I was in that same gloried Cathedral under the same Dome signing, Elgar's, the Angel Chorus, "Praise to the Holiest in the height". It was quite hard for me not to let the tears roll.

The Royal Festival Hall, well in my vision and with my love for music, I lost no time in avidly attending concerts there. Then, just after a few years, with a friend's bright suggestion, I became one of the stewards at the Royal Hall. I think this was one of the best things I ever did for myself. I was getting huge platefuls of scrumptious music for my voracious hunger for it. I could now have large dollops of it more often in the week. It was a deeply precious privilege listening to brilliant orchestras and watching immaculately performed ballets. The added perks were seeing, meeting and talking to some very distinguished screen and television celebrities and even the Royals.

Another enjoyment of music was with the Music Club of London. We visited several venues of general interest like Winston Churchill's childhood home, the Blenheim Palace, and the Chartwell House, his home in later years. There were other interesting spots to visit, also for demonstration of great musical works. We attended Mozart's Cosi Fan Tutte performed at the famous Glyndebourne Opera house in Kent. On the way, we stopped at Anne Boleyn's Hever Castle.

I thought the garden was a Fairy Land, the Opera is hilarious but I certainly do not, at all, agree with Mozart. There was another day trip to this Opera House to see the grounds and the backstage goings on, the rehearsal and the Green Rooms and the exuberant costume collection. My most memorable evening with the Music Club was when we attended a Quartet Concert at a luxurious Stately Home. Before the concert, there was time to mill around in the beautiful grounds where we were served drinks and tit bits by servers in their period costumes. Inside, it all was super grand. That evening, the late Queen Elizabeth the Queen Mother was also present, and our seats were just behind hers. During the interval, she turned around and had a good chat with us; she had no airs about her. What a lovely, truly gentle lady!

Now, how can I not write about the Scrabble bug that was turning twisting and gnawing inside me! I just had to find someone and somewhere to play; I found the answers at our library, on the reception desk. There were leaflets asking people to join the Inter-Varsity Club. It was offering variety of activities, including Party Evenings, Weekend dancing, visiting numerous wonderful sights and places, quizzes and of course, Scrabble. I joined the club. This was yet another good thing that came my way, I wanted to make the most of most of whatever my fingers could get into. Amongst other things, the House Parties were full of fun and laughter. I enjoyed visiting numerous parts of Natural Beauty and landmarks of ancient derelict and modern structures. England is an amazing country, full of nature's grandeur and man-made complex creations. O, please do not spoil this land.

Talking of landmarks, every time I see in real, or on the television or even a picture of the Big Ben, I'm deeply reminded of going on tour of the Houses of Parliament. We went in and out of all the doors and corridors in the palatial building. Then, into the House of Commons and in the House of Lords. We saw the throne where her Majesty the Queen sits when on her duties there. We saw the leather seats where all the attendees sit during Her presence or at other times. The most exciting of it all was going up the endless stairway leading to the clock at the top of the newly named Elizabeth-the-Second-Tower. We arrived in the colossal room containing the clock mechanism, and the engineer there showed us how he has to balance a penny on a cog to keep the times accuracy. The bell itself is enormous, like a huge hillock hanging on a hook. Then thunder struck; it was just time for the bell to strike. The floor beneath us actually rattled. And the sound? more like a billion drums simultaneously drumming. Stepping out on to the balcony, looking down, we saw ants and beetles rushing on a silvery ribbon way, way down below. The view over London was magical.

With all the treasure of new experience, my own luxury at the club was laying my hands on the Scrabble board. There were several evenings of it, I did not miss any! It was good to have many other similar enthusiasts. The greatest glory of it was that I won all my games, and that earned me a nickname. I became the club's Scrabble Queen! O, what a laugh! When for the first time, the National Scrabble Championship was launched, and I had no notion of it, someone most thoughtfully brought an application form, and strongly insisted that I should fill and send it in. With a lot of no, no and yes, yes, I did send it in. I was not going to lose anything in doing so. I received a response to my application and I was directed to play two games with someone appointed by them. I was so excited; even losing might not have mattered but to my delight, I won both my games with fairly good scores. What I had not even remotely expected happened. To my extreme delight, I was one of the very first 100 contestants to play for the National Scrabble Championship. My name amongst a few others appeared in the local newspaper; I was bursting with excitement and could not wait for the day. The longer I waited, the further drifted the date; finally we were there.

The games were fixed to be played at the prestigious Grosvenor Ballrooms on Landon's elite Park Lane. The setup was palatial with a huge chandelier and general luxurious decor in the huge hall. Contestants were assigned to play three games against different opponents. I won all my three games with fairly good scores. At the end of the games, was put up a board with our final total scores and positions, I had not in my faintest dream I had not expected to be right at the top, well I was not. Argh! Still, I was chuffed with myself to stand tenth from the top, leaving ninety behind me. On the whole, the day was wonderful, full of fun and laughter. I had yet more laughter in store for me when during one of the games, my opponent thought I had mis-spelt a word and 'challenged' me. Of course my word was valid and was passed by the dictionary.

The next day, the newspaper gave an account of the National Scrabble Championship – where it was played and how many played and how the game went on. At the end, they included some of the most uncommon and unusual words that were played. My word that was challenged 'saury', was amongst them. Saury is a fish; I had not spelt 'sorry' incorrectly.

I came up to be a contestant for a few more years. I have lost track of my positions, though. Matches were played at different and just as exotic venues like the Grosvenor Ballrooms. From the National Championships, the London Scrabble Club evolved, games were arranged to be played at members' homes making these evenings more enjoyable. Now, I was having a greater thrill of visiting and seeing more and more of beautiful London, and my fill of playing Scrabble. If you want to be happy playing a game, forget Snakes And Ladders forever, and take my advice, discard the cards, chuck the Chess and ditch the dice. Just play the game to play, Scrabble.

Travel and Sights

With all my climbing jumping and running around, I also had in me the 'naughty boy', that John Keats had written about. *"There was a naughty boy and a naughty boy was he. He ran away to Scotland the people there to see." With 'him', in me.* I had a great love for travelling and for seeing as much of the world as and whenever it was possible. School holidays were open gates and I made the most of those times. Looking back, I feel great! Seeing how much of the earth's surface I have covered, mostly in the Northern Hemisphere. Starting in India – a vast country with different topography, and like all the other places, people with different beliefs and varied ways of living. My first Summer school holidays, after I started working, were in Darjeeling, a beautiful hill station in the Himalayas. There – the air much cooler and purer. From the hotel where I stayed, I could see the snow-covered Mount Everest. It looked so near; I could touch it. It's great spread in stillness filled me with deep awe and unbroken calm. There it lay in all its undisturbed glory and majesty.

Hill stations were the place to be during the Summer months, as it became too hot down in the planes. I am happy to have holidayed in several of them like Nainitaal, Saattal, Massoori and Shimla which was the British government's

Summer headquarters. Boating in the small pleasure boats on the Dal Lake in Kashmir was great fun. The added enchantment of going to the hills, was getting up there, riding the very narrow-gauge train, zig zagging in the sloping sides of the hills sometimes touching the edges of the cliffs with vast hollow down below. Chugging along, it felt like having a joy ride in a toy train in a Theme Park. My! What an experience!

Ever since I was at school, I had deep dangling dreams wishing someday to go abroad. Having lessons in English and so much Englishness around, not surprisingly, England had become my main target. I am happy to have eventually made it. England in itself so full of amazement makes a marvellous centre point for visiting other places. In the earlier years, together with my sister and Brother-in-Law, we went to visit Edinburgh, Scotland. All these new places for me; at that time, were like being completely in another world and to me were great eye opener. I remember the moment; I was awestruck seeing the floral clock deep set in the ground and the blooms filled, the hands, functioning perfectly to utmost accuracy. The castle was just as awe inspiring, nestled in such height. On another holiday in Scotland, I was in the Isle of Bute. For a day trip, we were boating on Loch Lomond – a vast expanse of water. It was just like being on the sea again. We had heard stories of the elusive Loch Ness monster and laughingly wondered we might see something like that here too. I had my eyes wide open, just in case! All I could see was the breath-taking scenic beauty all around.

My experience was similar in Cardiff in Wales. The Town Hall seeped in grandeurs. My special memories are of being at the Welsh Folk museum. What an ingenious way of preserving the past brick by brick. The little chapel built perhaps just for two.

The whole of our little island is full of amazing spots, both natural and man-made. The southern coastal places have their own unique charm with the Blue Pool and the ancient rocks. In Cornwall, a quarry turned to the Eden Project is quite a thrill and it is thoroughly thriving.

On another holiday, I visited the southern island of Jersey. In a way it was exciting. I stayed at the Victor Hugo Hotel. Not quite a four star one, I could be stirring my tea with a coffee spoon but that did not matter. I was elated having my room next to the one where the famous novelist stayed. I presume he wrote his *"Les Miserable"* here. And other venues where entertainment shows were conducted. One evening, Paul Daniel was on, showing his amazing mind-boggling tricks. Afterwards, I even met up with him and boldly asked how he did those acts. He promptly diverted. I still think it was good fun talking to him. He was jovial and light hearted.

Another of my most memorable time there was a 'get up and go' adventure. I had overheard of the Guernsey Flower Show and that was the very day it was on. In the spur of the moment, I hurried myself to the airport, where a plane was ready to take off. I got on it and just a short flight, I was where all the hub hub was. There in all their beauty were the flower laden floats. They came in all forms and sizes. Millions of blooms decked in decoration of all possibilities. Their scent ascending to the resounding sounds of music and the cheering all around on the ground. The air filled with joyous gladness was just heavenly. Float after float, they kept on coming. I stayed there till quite late, reluctant to get to the port to get in the boat sailing back to Jersey. This is one of my most cherished memories and a totally pleasant one.

London, England makes an open passage to our next door neighbour – Europe. My first visit there was to Lugano, Switzerland. Our hotel 'Calypso' was not very far from the vast lake. I was mesmerised by the gigantic fountain in the middle. It spluttered water to an unbelievable height. It was great just being beside this vast vastness of water. Switzerland is known to be a beautiful country and I was excited to be standing on European soil yet again. Here, I also experienced a ride on a Funicular, it was exciting gliding down the slope.

Over the years, I have been to many other countries, and have enjoyed travelling, seeing the different people in their own ways of living. I will never forget being in Oberammergau for the Passion Play. Our stay there was arranged in nearby people's homes. That itself was marvellous, experiencing the local hospitality. The Sacred Play is performed every ten years now, and takes several hours in action. This is done as a promise people had made to God. Many years earlier there was an intense spread of plague. The villagers prayed to be set free of this gross disease. Their prayers were answered and the plague vanished. The people, in gratefulness took a vow to remember Christ's life, as a token of thanks to their Saviour. The actors prepare themselves for serval months. The costumes and the scene are made to make look 'real'. The performance specially the depiction of Christ's Passion, and His Crucifixion are solemn and breath-taking. Peoples' diligence and deep devotion are hugely admirable.

After this wonderful and awe-inspiring experience, we were in Voss, Norway. I loved seeing a shop where violins were made with intricate workmanship. Then of course boating in and out of the Fjord was exciting, with the unique scenic lay out. Still in Norway, in Bergen we visited Grieg's house and saw his piano, from which all his beautiful music oozed.

My brother and I were in a small Danish island. We wanted to visit Copenhagen. One early morning a ferry, then a long coach drive we were in the Capital. We looked around a bit, but both of us were very keenly eager to see the Little Mermaid, made famous through the enchanting Fairy Tale. We asked here and there to know where it was. I was looking for a high plinth on which she might be seated.

To our deep dismay, to begin with, we did not even notice her. Then, O, there she was! Looking unkempt, by the very rugged edge in water covered in green slime. That was a dreadful disappointment, but at least we had seen her. To make up for the let-down, my thrill came from crossing the wide vastness of water and the very long unending bridge, coming back to our small Danish island.

Holland is an amazing place. What an example of human conquest over nature. Most of that land reclaimed from the deep sea! and now filled with windmills and wooden clogs! Then what contrast! My wonderful vision of miles of flower fields, filled with blooms of all colours and hues.

I was similarly enchanted by the scenic beauty of Slovenia and Croatia with their unique topography.

On a fortnight cruise on the Baltic Sea, it was interesting passing through the Kiel Canal. We stopped in Tallinn and Sweden, but my most memorable time was in Russia in St Petersburg, a world in its own. We visited Catherine's Places. How fabulous! All drenched in gold, and in one room every bit covered with amber; pictures, amber mosaic. The vastness of buildings and the onion-shaped domes were most impressive. In Helsinki, Finland, we visited the House of Sibelius. How bewildering to think he composed all his music without the use of an instrument. He did not have a piano. One was given him much later. When he felt inspired, he'd take himself to a quiet room, with his favourite cigar and specially chosen ashtrays, and create his score. We were pleasantly treated to listen to his most famous work, his key signature, the Finlandia. It was played on a piano with beautiful intonation, and perfect effects. I have never heard it rendered so superbly. My spirits were dimmed seeing the memorial erected in his commemoration which seemed to have nothing musical about it.

Perhaps my eyes could not see it.

Finland is full of lakes. In another holiday, there four of us were in Tampere, our hotel which had been some years before a paper mill, was just beside a vast lake. It was wonderful walking beside it and watching people doing their normal chores. What I most enjoyed in Tampere was going to the Central Park with some children's attractions there. Amongst the few shops was a tower housing a rotating restaurant and, that's where I had to be. We had scrumptious tea and delicious ice-cream, going round and round up in the air. But for me, this was not the first time in a rotating restaurant. While visiting a friend in Berlin, Germany, she took me to the one there; it's a marvellous experience seeing the scenes changing every second. I quite enjoyed being in Berlin, seeing the most famous Gate and it was great fun being at the Check Point Charlie.

Talking of going right up, how exciting it was to be high up on the Eiffel tower in Paris, an inter-woven structure of solid steel. All my life, I had heard of it, seen its pictures and had marvelled at its size and shape. Now, I was actually on it, right up high with gorgeous views around, but then, what of being way, way down in the depth, deepest under the sea. Yes! This was a travel. Two of my friends and I made to Europe through the Channel Tunnel. I was quite intrigued travelling under the river Thames on the underground, how amazing it was fathoms deep under the sea! What a tremendous feat of engineering! We spent a few days in Bruges, Belgium. There the wows! Seeing the colossal buildings surrounding a spacious central square. On one side of it, numerous horse carriages waited to be engaged. We visited a chocolate factory, quite a small one but at least they let their secret out. My huge amazement, and lacking dexterity in my own hands, anything like that makes me deeply struck with wonder. This was a group of women making intricate laces, not on posh machines but seemingly simple contraptions formed of just a few knobs. They would pull this one and that one this way and that. How did they keep track of which one to pull next ? To me, it was all a muddle. From that tangle, the outcome was the creation of such beautiful handiwork. How could I not be spellbound?

Another capturing one was the King Wenceslas Square in Prague, Czech Republic, with a gigantic statue reigning over the lining shops and stalls. At the other end, a high building housed a clock with intricate amusing small figures that danced and displayed their play as the time chimed. A vast crowd gathered to see the scene. From the square, a path leads to the great gurgling river covered by the famous bridge which, on either side has statues of honourable and memorable names of distinction. What an experience of walking on ancient history!!

Height, and depth deep under the sea! I'll never forget the deep, deep depth down under a mountain. From the outside it was unbelievable that these solid rocks composed a crowning canopy for the tremendous treasure chest underneath.

A short narrow path led to the opening to the immense wonder, one more of nature's mouldings. This is Nerja, Spain, a colossal Cathedral carved in cavernous cave. Millions of years work by the drop by drop dripping water forming the fabulous stalactites dangling from the ceiling, and on the ground, the stalagmites making an effort to grow upwards. Each column moulded with precision, with prefect pattern and lacy designs. Jaw dropping or what! Nature's wonder never cease and all for our enjoyment.

In Italy, yet another cavernous eave full of water. With an extremely small entrance not on terra ferma, but by a little boat into the blue lake. A vast emptiness containing crystal clear water, cradled in deep blue, bluer than the blue of a blue corn flower. This was the magic of minerals deep in the bed being reflected through the water's clarity.

Italy is an amazing country. Boot shaped peninsula built of scenic topography seeped in ancient cultural and religious history. In Rome, of course, the Vatican City made a grand centre point to visit. All the Papal spaces and the monumental Cathedral cannot be missed. Inside it, immediately one feels the deep sense of calm. I was shakenly impressed by the spectacular insides of the Sistine Chapel. It does not seem real it does not look as if done by human hands, pictures painted on the ceiling! the painter dangling upside down!

I also loved it by the Trevi Fountain; in itself a structural feat. People throwing their coins making wishes. I do hope all their wishes do come true.

The Colosseum, a big attraction, an ancient relic. It was very hard to imagine both the beast lions and men in the same place together. What a heart! that put them there, is unbelievable, unthinkable.

I was totally mesmerised in Milan. First a visit to the La Scala, a sophisticated sophistication of splendour. Layer upon layers of seating looking down on the wide stage, where the great music was played and great Operas performed. Then there was the super, spread out shopping arcade representing all the big names that luxury can spell.

The Milan Cathedral holds its own magnificence with many high spires and strong imposing frontage. My truest treasure was seeing Da Vinci's 'The last supper', thankfully it's well preserved in the old refectory.

The other Mediterranean islands are just as fascinating, open books of historical stories.

Crete has its own ancient episode. Rhodes was quite an awe, seeing the pillars still standing, where supposedly the legendary colossal Colossus stood. The pillars, many feet apart make the spot where his feet stood.

How gigantic the statue must have been!

Cyprus is also full of old relics and ruins. In Paphos, still exist the ruins of what was once a vast pagan temple. This is where St Paul was humiliated, bound to a pillar and brutally tortured. Part of that pillar still stands.

Further north, my eyes were opened, when I got the answer to my puzzle and a question I had in my mind for so long. What did Lazarus do when he was made whole again after having been dead for three days and laid lifeless in a tomb. Jesus simply asked him to come out from there. There Lazarus was alive and fully well. Lazarus then came to Cyprus, ministered to a great congregation. Those who heard him respected him. The Church where he preached, now stands bearing his name. He finally died in Cyprus.

While still in Cyprus, there was a day trip to Cairo, Egypt. An early breakfast was arranged and we left for the airport. A short flight landed us in the ancient city. A capacious coach carried us to the ageless pyramids. Not just the enormity but how they were constructed baffles me. Each colossal stone accurately cut and precisely placed. No machine, no elaborate tool just human ingenuity, diligence and devotion. Yes it was quite an experience standing by and looking up the tremendous structure. I felt the same awe seeing the Sphinx.

At the Cairo Museum, I felt as if enwrapped in strangeness, seeing the mummies of people who countless years ago, were once alive and going about doing their own things. I had a good hearty chuckle standing right in front of the gold moulded bust of Tutankhamun. I almost wanted to say, 'Hello, we've met before.'

Some years earlier, there was an exhibition of Egyptian paraphernalia in London at the British Museum. The gold bust was prominent; I had seen it there in exactly the same way, standing right in front of it. For a moment, it felt quite bizarre.

It was captivating watching them demonstrate how from the papyrus reed, our modern papers evolved. For me, the 'must have' was a picture painted in the style of and on Egyptian paper. Well, I have it and what more, my name is written in hieroglyphics. That makes me wonder, I had problem writing Urdu in school how did they fair at their work?

Finale of this marvellous trip was a few hours cruise on the river Nile, late in the evening, with sprightly music, colourful belly dancing and food galore to match.

The other islands I have visited are Lanzarote, revealing it's volcanic origins. Tenerife boasting its possession of the oldest in the world Yucca tree. But I think my favourite, the enchanting Madeira, with the very narrow and extremely steep roads. What a life clutching experience! coming down in a Wicker basket on an almost vertical road. Controlled by two white garmented men!! Once down, you could just but laugh and devilishly even want to do it again and again. An easier way going up in the cable car was just as exciting, drinking up the views.

The people in Madeira have their own unique charm with unceasing smiles, and singing, their amazing dancing and intricate spell binding lace making. The vegetables, fruits and flower markets full of fancy fare as if from a fairy land. I highly recommend a visit to Madeira, especially during the Yule Tide. The weather throughout the year is superb. No, you could not even vaguely dream of a White Christmas.

The island decks itself in most lustrous lights of all almost unimaginable shapes, still depicting the seasonal scenes. New year fireworks are a wonder of their own, filling the sky with blooming brightness popping way up high and raining drops of starlets. I loved all Portugal with its grand landscape, wide sea shores and white washed houses topped with intricate chimneys.

But the best, the very best still, was my holiday in Iceland, an anecdote in itself. I was extremely excited from the moment I had booked two weeks there in Reykjavik, and every moment since then turned out to be magical. My ignorance was playing a good part in it. I had visions of walking on ice covered grounds, why? The name says so! I was also visualising rows upon rows of igloos and masses of husky pulled sleighs. With this super vision, with my usual clothes, I also packed up my snow boots and some winter Woollies in my suitcase. Then all in the plane still surely expecting to land on blocks of ice! This is what ignorance does to you! We landed in Keflavík, the only International Airport in Iceland; from now, my ignorance started turning to huge surprise. My eyes opened seeing instead of blocks of ice, we were standing on deep brown firm ground.

I was to travel in a coach believing it to be carrying me to my hotel. I was extremely excited and the wonder of being in Iceland was quickly adding up. It was middle of pitch darkness yet there seemed to be no lights on the way for miles around. How was the driver sticking to the road? That's expertise! After quite a long drive, the coach dropped me at the Reykjavik Central Bus Terminus. Baffled! That was not my hotel. For a while I did not know what was going on. I was standing on an entirely new place among complete strangers. Suddenly I was startled as I heard my name called. I felt relieved. He was from the hotel and had come to collect two small families and me; we got in a van. I was a bit puzzled but enjoyed the ride to the hotel, a small family run, looked welcoming. Inside, almost like a school office, the reception was checking us in; first the families were checked in. When I got to the desk, his face fell and he started with, "I am very sorry, Miss Peters, we do not have a room for you tonight." What was I to make of that? He soon revealed, my appointed room had not been vacated, but an arrangement had been made for me to sleep in the guest room. What did I care, as long as I had a bed to lay my head on. I thought the guest room, was posh! a wide comfortable coziness for me to snooze on, and I did sleep lordly. My stay at the hotel was fixed for half board. The dining room, a very pleasant space and the food was laid buffet style.

Having slept well, I woke up in that beautiful room with charming decor. I came down for breakfast. There, good food galore on the table. I took my fill of cereal, sausages sandwiches and whatever else, and found a spot to settle down to devour it all. Just then through the door came in the owner of the hotel straight towards me. Beaming with broad smile with the usual "good morning" and how are you, she started pouring buckets full of apology for not having my room available when I arrived, but now it was vacant and all ready for me to move in. I thought Gosh! Apology for making me so cosy, but, still to crown it all, she further came out with an offer of compensation. What a kind gesture, she said I could have a free meal of my choice any day I like. How I felt then, I cannot quite put into words. This was a marvellous start to my holiday and greater wonders were yet to come. My given room was well appointed, beautifully set, with a comfortable cosy bed, and a wide window with super views.

This was Summer time weather, I went around in my usual clothes. The houses? Not ice blocks, but white washed bricks built. The walls well insulated for colder times. I was fascinated even to walk on the solid deep brown ground considering that geographically, quite recently it was buried deep under the surface. Every corner I turned was to bring amazement. In the previous night while approaching the hotel, the van passed by a huge building with a high spire all brightly lit up. This was just around the corner and I had to come and see it. This is fairly newly built vast church and makes an unmistakable land mark for Reykjavik. On Sunday, I attended the service, just to be present there. It was full of joyous atmosphere with beautiful hymn singing and friendliness.

I also noticed vast structures every here and there. I was puzzled as to what they were. These are enormous Vats containing geothermal hot water. In the morning, when I had my shower, the water came directly from these. Homes do not have heaters, but are supplied heating from this natural source.

On my further stroll around, I came to an out spread park. The brown volcanic earth, not being cultivable, good soil here had to be imported. How amazing! Tons and tons of it! Now big shady trees and fabulous flora, alien to Iceland and a lake with all kind of aquatic living!!

On a day trip we were shown around an enormous treehouse gardening covered with tropical flowers, plants and trees. Bananas growing in Iceland!! This is the way the island uses the natural sources of warmth and the abundance of natural resources.

Several excursions were to the immense nature wonders. We walked on the slopes of a mute volcano, wandered by the magnificent Gullfoss, the golden falls cascading thirty-two meters over two thresholds. And then my most eagerly awaited for, at the Geyser, geothermal field where the little Strakkur erupts with steams and boiling hot water at intervals of about five to ten minutes. It gushes to rise sky high. In a jiffy, it falls, flop and then there's nothing.

It was an education! When we were shown some short column shaped stones, set in a semi-circle. This spot is where the world's very first parliament met and cultivated a culture of parliament in other countries.

I can never forget having a dip in the Blue Lagoon, a sprawling lake, yet another natural wonder! With constant warm water full of health beneficial minerals. It was such a marvellous unique experience I could have stayed on and on but time plays such impish tricks? It stretches like a rubber band when waiting for a bus or when waiting to see the love of your heart. But contracts like the pupil of your eye when you are in the brightness of having fun! I had to leave, the coach was out there.

My exceeding ecstasy was on the day trip to Greenland. I was to fly there. After breakfast, the taxi came to take me to the Reykjavik Domestic Airport. It looked more like a small bus terminus. I was bewildered, how can this be an airport. I just had to enquire three or four times to make sure I was in the right place. There were not many people around and the hub of an airport was seriously lacking. I felt I was in a cocoon, yet enjoying this unique mystery. Not for long tough. I was soon to be pulled out of this mist. My name was called and I was in the school bus! Well! that's what the little 'toy' plane looked like or a grass hopper perhaps? The sight of the plane added to my thrill. We were only ten or fifteen people on this trip. The plane was complete with an experienced pilot and a very friendly hostess. The plane took off and we were charmingly plied with coffee, cakes and cookies. I had taken my seat beside a window, to be able to look out down, and feel the height. Soon, we were over the sea. On it myriads of floating ice blocks to me they looked more like blocks of cotton wool. This view was enchantingly magical.

Not long, we landed on the south east coast of Greenland. Our passports checked, we came out and yet to my ignorant shock and surprise, we were not walking on solid ice, but surer then sure, on pure brown firm earth. The air not cold but comfortable. For far, it was just bare land lapped by the sea. In a short time we were in a dwelling and no igloos in sight, here also the small houses strong brick built! No huskies! The dogs are taken to smaller island, where they are rested fed and trained for the forth coming ordeal in the freezing cold season. The only outlandish thing I had seen so far and truly Green landish was the large fishes hanging like the washed washing on a clothes line. We were taken to a small Church, which was like any other anywhere, with pews, the altar with candlesticks, and flower vases. It was the same seeming familiarity in a grocery store. Why! I could have been standing in one in London! The same style of set up and the same fare, fresh fruits and vegetables, cereals, biscuits, chocolate, sugar, rice, flour and all the toiletries. I had to remind myself I was not in London, but in a remote Greenland. The old history books told of kayaks and spears used for fishing. There were no kayaks on the water but modern boats anchored on the shore line. Just for a treat and a glimpse into the past, an old man was asked to demonstrate how fishing was done. He was well apt in his act and in a dingy kayak showed exactly how a spear was used to spear a fish. As he went along, he sang a song in his own jolly lingo.

We were now at the end of our look around and were led back to departure. There the same plane was waiting for us, of course just like a school bus would have done. So the same pilot and the same friendly hostess. I took my window seat and well settled to look down from the height. We took off and just then the pilot in a contented voice announced that he had some spare time on his hand, and that he'd fly us over a longer route over the hills and meadows. This was absolutely sweet music to my ears; we were flying way above the mountains, covered in layers and layers of snow, and the layers broken into deep fathomless crevasses. Had a giant left his deeply icing-sugared cake cut to pieces? What an unforgettable panorama! We were back in Iceland and the day trip in Greenland, like a dream of a fairyland.

My short stay in Iceland had been full of intrigue, marvellous mystery and wondrous wonder. I could have gone on staying in such a magical place, where even the sun did not want to go down! Gladly my big treat was still waiting for me; I had to have my promised meal. I deliberately kept myself a bit hungrier, how crafty!! and spruced myself to match and mingle with the elite. It was quite late in the evening the sun still at its best, full bright, and gleaming. I sat myself at a table in the posh set dining room. The waiter showed me the menu. Every letter in it was double Dutch, well Icelandic to me, and did not mean anything, so he smilingly pointed at the priciest item. And promptly brought it. The dish was mostly fish. I loved it and polished off the plate. Well-fed and brim full of gratitude. The people at the hotel were friendly and I had the most wonderful time staying here. I consider it to be the best holiday I have ever had.

One of my cousins was living in Canada, way up north in Churchill. Several times, she had asked me to go there to see the polar bears just outside houses looking for food. I could never make it there. What a miss! Once Summer, she with her husband and daughter were in Toronto. Yes, happily I could make it there, a lovely place, not far from the land mark The C.N Tower all lit up in the night. Of course, I had to make a bee line for it. Once inside and in the lift, in a blink of an eye and we were right up on the very top. The views around were gripping and down below just dots and spots!!!

The extremely wonderful experience was at the exuberant Niagara Falls. Just the sight of it is an unexplainable sensation. I was ecstatically all excited seeing the unstoppable, enormously colossal, roaring, thundering cluster of falling water. What more! We went in those waters in a boat the 'Maid of the Mist.' This was actually, not just near the cascade, but right behind the vast liquid wall. We had to put on waterproof cloaks. That thundering roar and the gushing splashes made an experience like that of being on another planet, yet undiscovered.

The Niagara Falls make an unparalleled unmatched thrill. The roar kept on roaring and the falls kept on falling creating a more exuberant sight till late into the night, when the whole scene becomes magically all lit up with bright colourful lights changing like dancing steps. This has been one of my greatest joy, excitement and the gigantic thrill of my days.

In Canada, we also visited Ottawa and, explored the seat of government. In Quebec, the French influence is well apparent.

To come back to London, I had to fly from Winnipeg. We drove all the way from Toronto, passing through other interesting places amongst them, the great lakes.

After completing her Ph.D. from the Columbia University in New York, Catherine had been living there. She made suggestion to go and spend some time with her. I had to find ways. The golden chance came through the club 'Intergrad' I was a member of. Our flights to New York and back were arranged. All through these years, I had kept in touch with my dear Miss Collins, who was now retiring in a Missionaries Care Home in Pasadena, California. She told me of Grey Hound Coach Services, an easy way to go around in the States. I equipped myself with a ticket which would allow me a month's travel. The coaches are a bliss with very comfortable reclining seats. The coaches could be boarded whenever and wherever the coach was bound for. Another of my big dreams was coming true.

We arrived in New York. Catherine came to receive me. It was good to see her again after a long time. I was absolutely delighted being in America. I spent about a week with Catherine during which she took me round to see some of the spots I was keenly eager to see. I took in a show at the famous Radio City Hall and saw the Juliard where our music director at collage had graduated from; visited the Lincoln Centre; wandered in the vast Macey's Store, walked in and out of the surrounds of the tall towering Sky Scrapers and of course the most enchanting, the Empire State Building. It had been a fascination of mine from my childhood. We had a book at home titled "The wonders of the World". The book, amongst the pictures of many other mind-blowing wonders had one of this very high structure. It had been described fully. Both John and I would gasp trying to visualise the height. Our necks bent right back and pointing upwards O, it's way up there!! Now with that memory, I was actually standing beside it, my neck bent right back again, and I could see the real top way, way up there! Seemingly touching the sky, shrouded in mist and clouds. And what do you think? of course I had to go up to the top. A very fast lift got me there. How exciting! At the top of the world!!! The earth almost invisible and whatever could be seen down below was just a pin point.

After a week in New York, I was deeply looking forward to, all on my own, well geared for my sojourn in the Greyhound. I wanted to make the utmost of my travel around, and pack in as many places as my time would allow. My account is not in any particular order.

Catherine came to see me off on my long adventure. I was to spend some days and nights travelling in the coach and staying at small hotels overnight in places where I got off.

In San Francisco, my stay was not very long. But I made sure I went on the full expanse of the Golden Gate Bridge. This is how handy the Greyhound is! I was not to spend any time on the other side so I got back to look around and in and out of the shops. Being on the bridge was thrilling with all the scenes from there.

I was very glad to be in Boston. I eagerly visited the University grounds where Catherine had studied before going to the Columbia University. I was also most interested as our Isabella Thoburn College in Lucknow is a 'Sister Institution.' I felt good being in Boston. In a big park, there was a lake and I enjoyed going on it in a swan shape boat. However, the biggest 'must do' there, was going to the Harvard University to see the highly recommended Glass Museum. How very astonishing and mind-blowing!! specimens in every show case. These are models of every flower and plant collected from far and near; abundant or rare. Every petal, every sepal, every corolla, every leaf and every stem modelled to perfection in glass! Every colour or hue, every form, size and shape moulded to such accuracy to look as if newly, freshly handpicked from the garden; all extremely marvellous and breath-taking.

I spent three most wonderful days in Nebraska where I stayed with a couple who had every dearly endeared Catherine and made her feel 'at home' with them. I happily felt the same. One morning, I was taken to the local Newspaper Reporter's Office. I was asked to tell a little about myself. I said I was with my friends visiting Nebraska and I'd been travelling on the Greyhound. Originally from India. I now lived in London where I've been teaching in Secondary Schools. All this made an interesting point. The next morning, there I was! A full-size picture of me on the front page of Nebraska local newspaper together with my story. My fame at last! At home, I felt spoilt drowned in welcoming tender homeliness.

From Nebraska, I travelled to Salt Lake City, Utah. There to visit the Mormon establishment was a must. On the way, the coach driver made a deliberate short pause by the Mount Rushmore, so that we could have a good view of the world famous-carving of the four past presidents of the United States. We arrived very early morning on the Sunday at the Temple Square; the gatemen still looked sleepy. They had a little chat with me. In the grounds, the vast Tabernacle with its high spires looked awe inspiring. I roamed around the museum of Joseph Smith, the founder of the Mormons, The Church of the Latter Day Saints. I was shown inside a building all decked with the most beautiful elaborate pictures of biblical scenes. The highest high light for me was attending the morning service in the huge church, with a colossal organ and a multitude of choristers. The service was solemn, and the choral singing raised praises filling the air. All this had been a most wonderful, impressive experience for me. God moves in mysterious ways to show His wonders.

In California, at her suggestion, I just had to go and visit Miss Collins in the Care Home. I was so delighted seeing her again. Now, in the Missionaries' Care in the U.S., she looked a lot frailer, but was just as warm and mumsy! With a friend of hers, she took me around to look. I saw the glaring Hollywood sign on the side of a hill, we stopped and listened at the Sugar Bowl where Zubin Mehta was rehearsing his orchestra. The sound was great.

It was wonderful and deep joy being with Miss Collins again and being under her mumsy wings.

So, saying a Good-Bye was a dreadful wrench.

While still around there, going to Disneyland was an essential. O, what a place! A true fairy land.

How enchanting! going on the rides and seeing all those fascinating shows, hilarious and totally outlandish! I was a little wilful child again!

I say, Disneyland is not just for the young ones but also for the teeny toddlers, teenagers and 'ties agers as well, it's a must see spot.

On all my long travels on the Greyhound, I made several stops for refreshment or just to stroll around for fun, in nearby spots, not really for anything particular. I have to mention Albuquerque, again not because I did anything special there, but just because I like saying it. Go on, you say it!! Albuquerque, I bet it will make you chuckle!!! From here, I made my way to the Grand Canyon. My! What a sight, what a view!!! The enormous gorge with a depth, equalling the height of a high mountain. The hilly steep sides of the vast hollow, looked as if deliberately hand painted in numerous colours, forming a mind boggling Kaleidoscope. This was another breath-taking experience.

I had been on these coaches, all on my own, and for so many days, making it a totally novel adventure. Still, I wasn't quite done yet. I was to call in Washington, D.C. and there, the greatest of great co-incidences!! I was arriving in the Capital, the same day, as my brother John and sister-in-law were. John had been selected by the English Speaking Union, as an "exchange", to teach in Austin, Minnesota. Washington, D.C. Was his initial 'Welcome'. They were in the Capitol building, where I was to see them. Gee!!! All excited, I felt great even stepping on the façade, then on the steps and through the decked corridors, where my brother was waiting to see me. It was enchantingly marvellous seeing them again, and in this out-of-the world place. What more, Catherine came over as well from New York. The four of us together again after a long time. All of us went looking around. At the White House, we photographed ourselves, with the garden and the fountain in the background. I'm sure, that must be a favourite spot for all the tourists and visitors to have their pictures taken.

The high light in Washington, D.C. was going to the famed Smithsonian Museum – another eye-bobbing, jaw dropping experience. There, taxidermy at its highest peak, and the craftmanship in excellence of arranging the showcases, nearest to looking natural. It looked that the monkeys would jump to another branch any moment; that the penguins would start waddling, and that the tiger would snarl and snap at you. It all was quite amazing.

Our time being together was soon coming to an end. John and my sis-in-law were to be back at their spot, and Catherine and I travelled back to New York.

My past few weeks, at all the places, which so far, were only mentioned in books or shown in pictures, I now had been to, and actually seen myself. It all was like a wild dream. This was an experience I could have never thought of or imagined I'd ever have. Even to this day, going over the Golden-Gate Bridge in San Francisco, standing by the Grand Canyon, looking down from the Empire State Building, boating behind the Niagara Falls and being amazed by the hot springs Strakkur in Iceland, all seem like a deep dream.

I spent few more days in New York before flying back to England. Still, this was not the last Good-Bye to USA. I was to get back there many more times.

Few years later, my sister Emily and I were in Kissimmee, Florida to go on a cruise on the 'Carnival' boat 'Fantasy'. A four-day luxurious trip around some of the Caribbean Islands.

The boat itself, a floating palace; the evening shows most entertaining, with colourful costumes; in the days unmissable displays of carved fruits, vegetables into unthinkable shapes and an exhibition of a huge block of solid ice block turn into an entirely new image within minutes. This was an unforgettable holiday hugely enjoyed.

But my visits to America were not yet complete. My younger sister, Mercy, lives in a beautiful home in Dallas, Texas. I spend my Christmas there with her. But, it was not even to her, I came back again and again. Why? I'll soon reveal.

Getting into Publication

Things were happening to me in the most wonderful ways. I had been through amazing experiences, I had never thought of or dreamt I'd ever be in. There I was, seeing the spouting springs at Geyser in Iceland or being splashed at by the Niagara falls or even be standing, looking down the deep gaping gorge at Grand Canyon. New doors kept opening and I was feeling like a little girl in a Fairy Tale who had entered a vast opulent palace with gem-covered corridor and dazzling doors, and as she walked by, the portals flinging open just by magic.

From the early days, I had loved singing and reciting Nursery Rhymes, but had never thought one day I'd have some of my very own. I do not know when exactly my poems started, nor do I have the talent to tell myself to sit down and write one. They just happen to me quite out of the blue. Sometimes, when I have no expectation or even an inkling. Whichever way, my simple poems have happened, I've enjoyed writing them, and having them published, has been a "doors kept opening" experience.

My very first poem in print was in India, written after attending a YWCA holiday in Simla. The words were all the fun and laughter we had. The magazine included those lines.

The next were the two in our Methodist Church paper, I have already mentioned earlier. Still the thought of having my poems in books and anthologies never swept my mind. All that did happen and happened by chance.

I had a few poems in my book, never seen or read by anyone else. My best friend among the teaching staff, was the peripatetic Music Teacher. One day as we were talking, I do not know what I said but she snapped, "O, you sounded so poetic, you must try and write poems." At that, I laughed and told her that I had written some simple ones. She insisted on seeing them. She liked them and remarked that I should have them published. I took it as a jest but little did I know that from this point the 'doors' will start opening for me.

Up to now, I had never taken any notice of the invitation, we teachers had in our special newspaper to attend weekend seminars. These would be intensely informative and interesting. I did not know what I was missing, until somehow something pulled me to this particular one. We were about ten or twelve of us in it. The weekend really did turn out to be a wonderful experience. The theme was 'So you can be an author.' The seminars were fun enough but meeting other people was the cherry on the cake. By now, I was feeling crushed. Why I hadn't attended some of the other weekends I could have gone on, but felt delighted to have had the joy of being on this one. The relevant educational information we were receiving was all well sugared up. One seminar started when we had to look at someone and say the first thing that came to mind. In my turn, I looked at a gentleman opposite me and said, "I think of Oscar Wilde's 'Happy Prince.'"

That gentleman was the teacher's assistant at one of the schools in London. At the time of leaving, he very kindly announced and offered, if any of us had something that needed photo copying and duplicating, he'd do it. Back at school during the week, I was telling my friend how the Seminar was and what fun it all had turned out to be. I had met new people and had made new acquaintances. I laughed when I told her about the 'Happy Prince' and how good and kind he was. She immediately suggested that I should get my poems photocopied by him. She herself offered to type my work and insisted that I should take it to be worked at; she even designed a front cover and illustrated some of the lines. With her push and encouragement, I took the lot to 'The Happy Prince'. In only a few days, he had photocopied, collated and spiral bound several A4 sized books for me. How deeply grateful and delighted I was! Seeing my poems in a book form. My friend was also very pleased as it all happened because of her; she was the main instrument. In my vaguest dream. I had not realised that now I was on the threshold of another magical door. That door flung opened.

I was living in a block of flats. Opposite my room lived an elderly Jewish lady. She was very friendly and everyone who knew her called her, 'Auntie.' I very happily showed her my book. She was very pleased and on reading it, she highly complimented me. This was not all; in her Jewish Chronicle, she found an advert asking for poems Auntie at once egged me and insisted that I should submit one of my poems. Just to make her happy and to make her know I was listening to her, I yielded, and left at that.

A few days later, there it was! My poem in a proper Anthology through well-established publishing. I could hardly trust my eye, what I was seeing. I cannot express how excited I was. Perhaps it was the same way I felt in beating my Daddy at Lexicon when only a child of seven or eight. Now again, I wanted to go out and shout, "I have my poem in a book". I was showing it to any and everyone. The stream of wonder kept on flowing. My name was passed on to a compiler of a book titled 'Dear Mother', in presentation of that special day in March. Yes, my poem, "My Love" was in it. Very happily, my name was passed on yet again in turn to two other publishers and my poems were in these new anthologies. By now, I was getting used to seeing my simple words in proper print. By now, I had gathered enough gumption to make my own books and in turn I did two of them.

I was still in that long corridor where more new doors were yet to open. Once, when at the Royal Festival Hall, I wandered into the library there, just browsing, I found a leaflet asking for new poems. I responded with a sense 'let's see what happens.' I was thrilled when so unexpectedly my poem was accepted. This was the start of a river flowing of invitations for my poems by the same publisher and having several of my poems in their Anthologies, they compiled a small book with all my own poems. This was in a kind of acknowledgement and a gift to me by them. What a lovely present!

This was my third book.

Going back when my very first poem was in a book and I wanted to shout; well shout I did. With great excitement, I promptly picked up the phone to my sister in New York. "Guess what, guess what? I have my poem in a book." She congratulated me and expressed sisterly pleasure. In a few days, she was ringing me. In response to an advert she had seen, she asked me to send in my poem to the International Society of Poets. Goodness! I thought in America, my poem will not even be looked at. I completely ignored her words. She asked me again and again and I kept on turning a deaf ear. Then at last in a big sisterly firm compelling voice, she asked me again to send in my poem. That opened my eyes. I thought, well, I wasn't to lose anything and no one will know my poem came to no good, and I'd be able to say to my big sister that I obeyed her. Just to please her and quite accepting that my poem will not even be looked at, I sent one in. A few days later, I heard from America, to my stupendous surprise, that my poem was good. Not only that, to my great enchantment, a certificate was enclosed in the letter to signify my poem was among the Editor's special choice.

The dreamland opulent palace I was in, was truly fabulous! I kept on finding and collecting more of bright gems. Within a few weeks after the congratulatory letter, I received an invitation from the International Society of Poets to attend their Annual Symposium. This was extremely exciting. I was thrown into a real wonderland, and I could not wait. The symposium was to be held in the posh Hotel Sheraton in Washington, D.C. I could not miss that for anything. So back to the U.S this time not to sleep in the Greyhound coaches. At the venue, huge halls, colossal chandeliers and wide stairways all seemingly leading upwards and none coming down. My room was big with a double of double size bed and the wide window overlooked the expansive garden, all lit up with fairy lights in the night, how enchanting! All this grandeur was truly great, but greater grandeur was yet in store. In the evening, just before dinner, the lobby, decked with sumptuous array of flower arrangements beckoned us, where we mingled and formed new acquaintances, while being served drinks and tasty tit bits by charming waitresses. Then the dining hall doors flung opened with a massive crescendo of Fan Fare. Princely attired trumpeters marched down the vast hall lit up with colourful lights; we found our seats at the beautiful set tables for some two hundred attendees.

There was a warm welcome by the President.

Dinner was serval by the frilled, fairy like waitresses, soft music filled the air and Florence Henderson the screen actress graced us with her presence and entertained us with her jolly quips. Later, I had photograph taken with her.

Evening ended with more fun after dining. During the day, were the main happenings. In separate rooms, in smaller groups, each one of us was to read our poem, then we were adorned by a Poet if Merit medallion and an "Outstanding Achievement in Poetry" award. My very proud moment! The three days of the symposium were filled in some way or another with more poem reading, appreciating other's works and exchanging views; it all seemed to have culminated too soon. My sleeping on that very wide bed had ended but my stay in the US stretched on. I spent some time in Austin, Minnesota as a guest in the house, and with who had been the "exchange" with John. It felt strange being under the same roof where my brother had been. I was given the most wonderful time, then I was introduced to their dear friends, a most lovely couple. I was taken into their hospitality. I spent some exceptionally amazing time with them.

They were to take me on a trip in their car to show me around some more interesting places in the Mississippi region. In and out of huge and expensive restaurants, I was in a new world, my most memorable time with them was in Spillville. This is where, when he came to America, Antonin

Dvorak, the composer lived. His house is a museum of some of his belongings, including his piano, on which he made alterations and put finishing touches to his most famous work – 'The New World'. The house is very near the church where he was the organist at the services. Part of this house is also used to exhibit some of the most remarkable wood carvings. These were created by someone, who was from his very childhood got drawn to carving. At school instead of being attentive to lesson, he would be carving. He carved out the Nativity scene on his desk. The school did not reprimand him, but commended him for his creativity. The desk was kept as a prized show case item. The exhibition displayed some most intricate breath-taking sets. My favourite turned out to be the one of Jesus with his disciples, and one of a complete wedding. How impressive, and those intricately carved clocks!!

While in Spillville, we needed to spend the night in a hotel 'The Victoriana.' As the name suggests, the decor was very English, but what really got me was, when checking in, the receptionist asked me if I wanted a cat also, I was quite surprised, puzzled and thought it was kind of a joke. The receptionist explained that when one of the very regular clients is asked 'how he is', he always says 'he is very well, but he is so missing his little kitty'. The hotel caught the idea that there must be others with similar lacking. There now is a well-kept cattery of highly trained cats. Which are compatible to full fill the longings of those who so, so miss their little kitties. This, a total novelty for me, and what a super thoughtful consideration by the hotel.

In Kellogg, we visited a small goings on of some handicraft workshop. I bought a small set of Russian Dolls there. I absolutely loved these few days seeing so much more of America with such deeply dear, lovingly lovely people.

As I have indicated before, this also was not the last Good Bye to the US, but more of an au revoir, and many thanks to the Poetry Society. The next annual symposium was again in Washington, D.C. not at the Sheraton but at the equally luxurious Hilton. By now, I started feeling at home in Washington, D.C. I could be a resident there! The Society's doings were the same as before, more poetry reading to a large group, receiving the Poet-of-Merit, medallion and an 'Outstanding Achievement in Poetry' award and of course the fun and joy of mingling with many other poets.

One year the meeting was held in Hollywood.

The thought alone of going there was a bubble of excitement. All that was happening at the Renaissance Hotel next to the Kodak theatre. From my room window, I could see the great sign which, just a few years before, I had seen when driven around in a car. The format of the 'Poetry' was always the same but it was great being among many people and in such elegant venues. For me the bigger, added fun was walking down the Kodak Red carpeted steps on which the Fame had trod. I was led on to the Celebrity Star studded path. I made sure I stopped and stepped on each and every one of those famed names. What childish fun that was!! and I wanted to do it again and again.

Twice we were in Orlando, Florida; say Orlando and you dream of seeing the Water World, and the Universal Studios. Well, I did just that and who wouldn't? At the Water World, it was delightful seeing all the exotic creatures from close – a brilliant act from the dolphins, then the fun of the dread and the laughter on the rides. It was same at the Universal Studios with the acceleration of discovering the secrets of the fantastic film making like that of *Jaws*. These are the places where childhood returns with a bang and years forget where they stand.

The Poetry Society was held at the magical Disney Conference Centre. Everywhere Disney characters were implanted in pictures, models or even humans attired in Disney wear soaps wrapped in Disney paper and towels with Disney imprint. The whole atmosphere was enhanced by Disney presence, so full of fun and charm.

By now, several of my poems had been included in various anthologies. I felt deeply honoured by receiving a plaque, to say I was a Distinguished Member of the Society and twice received the honoured gold pin with the logo.

Most wonderful time was when the poets met in Las Vegas. Again, it was the same thrill and fun and joy of meeting others, making new acquaintances, reading poetry and sharing new views.

Las Vegas, the enchanting wonderland! We were not far from the central glamour. I explored some of these exuberant spots; even tried my novice hand at the fruit machine. Gingerly, I started with a miserly quarter. The device had pity on me, or was it playing a crafty trick. To begin with, by and by, my bucket was full of clattering coins. Every time I put my quarter in, there was a shower of them back. Should I have stopped there? But greed never pays! By and by as the bucket got filled, my quarter got devoured by the cunning machine and I was dry and empty again. My big enchantment there was seeing white tigers and the dancing splashing fountains in front of that palatial place.

Reading my poem in a vast room.

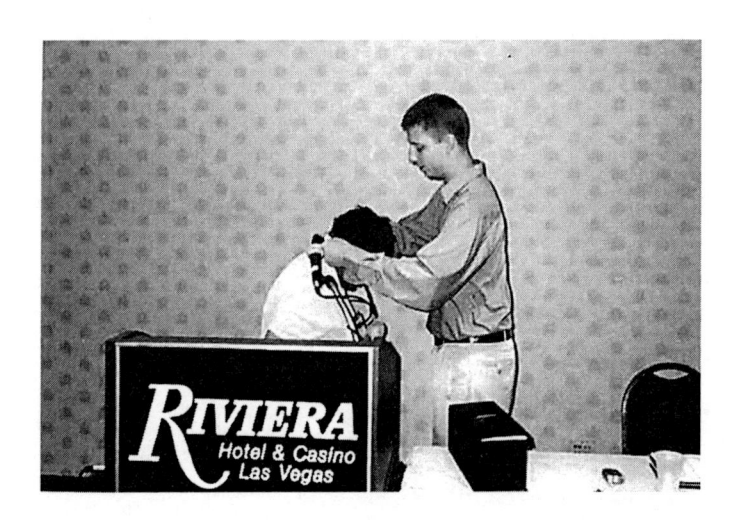

Receiving the medallion 'Poet of Merit'.

In the grounds of the Disney Conference Centre, with my 'Poet of Merit' medallion and my trophy.

All the poems I read at the symposiums and several others have been included in anthologies, made by the International Society of Poets, are now housed at the International Library of Poetry in Maryland.

I was also extremely excited when, seeing my poem, I had an invitation from the publishers in New York to print my work in their books.

In the meantime, with all my poems and the new ones, I have made a book of my own-the fourth one. It's CIP catalogue record is available from the British library, in London, England.

I feel hugely humble but deeply delighted to have shared my simple poems with so many people and to see them published in books. These books are housed in Maryland, New York, and in England.

My greater pleasure has been having my poems featured in Poetry Diaries, in several Best Poets and Poems of the Year books. My greatest and utmost joy is being featured in the International Who's Who in Poetry. My poem is the first on the front page leading the rest. This happened again the following year.

And, all this happened from a slight friendly remark, 'O, you sounded so poetic.'

From a tiny acorn, happened a wide wooded woodland.

I conclude my eventful life story by sharing some of my selected poems, mentioned earlier.

My Selected Poems
My Love

Mother,
I love you
For taking care of me
From the moment
I saw the first light.
You cradled me in your arms
Gently
And lulled me to sleep
With your lullabys.
You were awake in the night
At the slightest moan
That I made
To comfort me
Should I be in discomfort.
My tiniest tears
Were your giant pain,
My slightest smile and laughter
Your utmost again.
You saw me through life selflessly
It does not seem that long ago
When I was cradled in your arms with care
Now, as I stand on my own two feet
And, for all, for me you have done,
I love you with all my heart
And I always will
My beloved precious

Mum.

Dedicated to my most beloved Mother (step), Dr Ruth Nora Peters.
This poem was included in the book "Dear Mother", appropriately to celebrate the day in March.

The Sweetest Spot

On this wide, wide, wide earth
There's a little spot
I've loved the best
The spot where the sweetest flowers
Have grown with me
And the birds their sweetest carols
Have sung
Where the beauteous trees
Have lifted their arms above
As if to say their prayers
With me.
I think of the smiles
That were careless and free;
Of the tears that were
Seldom and rare;
Of the days that were vacant
Of any thought even of what
Tomorrow will bring.
Yet it was here
I had learnt to stand on my feet
It was here
I had seen the ways, of the world.
It was here
I took off the garb of childishness
And adulthood did me enfold.
You ask me the name
Of this sweet, golden place

Well I'll tell you
It's the haven of havens
The Queen Victoria at Agra.
I love it
And will always love it
O, the lovely spot
That's my dearest school
My Alma Mater
So good, so great, so true

England

England,
You land,
Seeped in mystery
Of rich ancient history
With dense battles won,
And many conquest done.
Where industry turned its first wheel
And medicine learned
The weakened to heal.
In your majestic, fascinating, old walls
Enclosing the big, vast halls
You hold wonder, grandeur.
Within them are played
Beethoven, Mozart
And, Wordsworth and Shakespeare
Breathed the great work of art.
England,
O, you little island
It's the very air
Surrounding you everywhere
That's makes you wonderous, mysterious
And man breathing it
Aspires to be great

The very first poem written in England, also included in the *New York Anthology*.

Will No One Hear

Silently sanding
Staring
At the stoutly shut gate.
Helpless, shuddering.
Tortured stiff
With tormenting fear.
Torn.
Ruthless weather
Is pouring numbing chill.
Furious, tearing gales of wind
Surround the unsurpassing
Quiet of the night.
Will no one hear?
Will no one turn a kind ear
To listen to the pleas
Ringing in the beggar's
Unspoken dreams?

The first poem in an anthology.
Thanks, Auntie!

To a Chestnut Sapling

Welcome little chestnut tree
You have just popped up
To say 'hello' to me?!!
Soon, high up you will grow
Leaving all else down below
Strong and sturdy
Rich in splendour
Yet, to the wind you will bow.
With sprawling branches
You will create a restful shade
In the noon day heat,
And the birds will knit
Their nests amongst you twigs.
The rain, the snow and the sunshine
Will snuggle on your soft leaves
And, the star sparkle
Will stream
Through your peep holes.
Chestnut tree,
Live and grow
In this wide, wide
Welcoming world
With me.

First poem published by the International Society of Poets with the Editors Special Choice (certificated).

The Lasers

Born to sing, to dance
Born into the unknown
Loose strings dangling
Like the tender tendrils
That take hold of the first thing
In the way, they find to hold.

Born to sing, to dance
Born into strangeness.
Strangeness of the air
That surrounds all around.

Then, life is a toddler
Exploring
Experiencing the vastness
Of the new world.
First, making one and one
To add up to
An immense three!
Until the mystery unravels
The truth and reality.

The world is full of lasers
Flashing in turn
Of darkness and light.
Worlds music swells and dims
While the dancing grows

Into the thunderous clatter
Of joyous rhythms
Of enormous claps of laughter.

Thus life goes on
The strains of music
Rise and fall
Like waiting
For new doors to open
And for greater opportunities.

Life is a bliss, a haven
Or, for some
This dance is unmanageable
And, the peals of music
A torment

Soon its late into the night
Last dance is announced,
Lights are dimmed,
Dancing ends,
The curtain falls
And the lasers
Are there no more

Published in the *International "Who's Who in Poetry"* on the first page, leading the rest.
Published by the International Library of Poetry, Maryland, U.S.A

Daffodils in a Vase

Daffodils
In a tall crystal vase
Bundled in bunches
Bursting with blazing beauty
Sitting
Sedately silent,
Yet each flower
As it opens
Speaks of things unspoken
Creating thoughts
Of hopefulness, gentleness;
Of love and kindness shown.
Sweet daffodils,
You will be my
Memory
Of all the days
Full of childish or foolish ways,
Sadness or joy, that like you
Will have come
And forever
Gone.

Published the following year in the *International Who's Who in Poetry*.
My poem is the first, leading the rest.
International Library of Poetry
Maryland, USA

The Chosen Twelve

They were twelve
Asked to follow Him,
Chosen, selected, hand-picked.
Denouncing their work, their home,
They followed Him.
Each picked for a commitment,
For a purpose to fulfil
One was chosen, handpicked, selected
For a deeper purpose to fulfil

In the eyes of the world
A betrayer a deceiver.

Was not the intent
Of the Father
That his only Son
Should be slain for our faults?
That He should suffer
Upon the cross
To pay up for our loss?
The cross is our redemption,
And our guilt
Is to bear
The blame.
It is our guilt, the betrayer, the deceiver
That caused
Him his pain.

Easter

Beloved of God
Heir to his glory
Loved us
He stooped down low
Making Himself equal with us.
But, man deep in sin
Was blind to this love
Given him by the highest
O, the cruel deep dark blindness
Which let not this love penetrate
Into the heart of man.
They despised Him wounded Him,
Made Him to bear the cross.
Then,
Buried him, making him
Slave to death.
But death had no power.
It could not hold him.
And, Jesus, glorious Jesus
Tore the gates of hell.
He is risen, risen from the dead
Conquering sin and hell
He is risen ever to live
Living to make us equal with him
For still, he loved us

"Greater love hath no man than this
That he should lay down his
Life for his friends"

First printed in the '*Indian Witness*', Methodist Church paper.

The Upper Room

Then, as a school girl
In imagination, all to surpass
I sat fast dreaming
In the Civics class.
I crept up the staircase
Of a colossal building –
The Upper House,
Frightened, lost and forlorn
Like a timid mouse.
My looks on either side
Of the banister
Met, with the framed, gaping stare
Of the long gone by politicians,
Whose names, though my books still did bear.
I crept up and upward still
To a heavy, deep carved ebony door,
To open a huge golden, knob it bore.
I turned it, opening the door
In the room I went,
Found a gigantic 'Round Table'
For the dignitaries themselves to present.
A hush descended
The conference began,
Quick turned my feet,
Frightened
Fast downward
I ran

Now in the same mystic
Imagination as I sit,
I can almost see myself
Climbing the staircase
That later led to Calvary.
I creep up and upward still
This time, though not to an ebony door,
I turn a knob, not a golden one
And those fantastic faces,
I see no more.
This is not the Upper House
But the Upper Room
Where Jesus knelt showing His friends
His father's kingdom.
He taught them in love
Washed their dirty feet
So, that they may learn
And obtain a Mercy Seat.

Now I run downwards,
Not with a fright
But, feeling the hold of His Hands.
So full of love and might.
These are the Hands of Jesus
Who to serve others
At all times, had taught us
Do we run from the 'call'
That bids us to serve,
And piles incessantly
Blessing from above?

First printed in the *Indian Witness*, the Methodist Church paper.

Praise Thee

When we can sing
With a voice, given free
Of our Saviour
Who reigns from above.
In the words of that song
He himself, does speak
Of His infinite love.

O, Master, our Ruler
Thou, forever would be
For, with our hearts
And voices
We shall sing of Thee

Bless us dear saviour,
On our daily path, as we go
So that we may love thee,
And praise thee
Now and Evermore

Dedicated to my beloved dad who was always singing hymns of worship and praise.
Some of his favourites were, 'Nearer my God to Thee', 'Holy, Holy Lord God Almighty' and 'O, Love that will not let me go.'

With Him Live...

For God so loved the world that he gave his only begotten Son, that whosoever believeth in him, should not perish but should have everlasting life. John 3:16

And, this 'begotten son' was Jesus.
From heaven He came to save us.
In a lowly home he took his birth,
To wipe away the sins from this earth.
He was laid in a manger.
While to the earth He was a stranger,

In depth of the night.
Shone a great light.
Of a star, awaring Wise men three,
In a faraway country
Of a poor little baby
Born to Joseph and Mary.
Following the star they came from a far, bearing gifts
To worship him and to adore him.

Some lowly shepherds, abiding in their fields.
Hurried to kneel beside him.
And to worship and adore him.

This baby grew in stature and in wisdom.
The people knew of his father's Kingdom.
For this little boy

Who must have played
With many a toy,
Now talked with doctors and priests
In the temple,
Of his father and His deeds.

He was always kind
To the sick and to the blind
He fed many with food.
And only went about doing good.

But men of this world.
In sin alone are bold.
They could not stand him,
And his righteousness,
Like a dark cloud
Cannot a star's brightness.
of Blasphemy they blamed him
Their only cry was
Crucify Him crucify Him.
Oh! This guiltless Jesus
To earth He came to save us.

It was then in Gethsemane garden, where all was calm, not a word spoken
But between him and his God.
He prayed for us all.
He had always done
His father's will
He loved him, obeyed him still.
Though his lot was bitter

The sword did glitter
That dreadful dark night
Devoid of all light.

Then, the cruel cross!
O, what a gross loss
He hung upon a tree
And died there
For you and me.

Came lightning and thunder.
They all trembled in awe and wonder
Our Jesus is no more
The tomb wide opened its door.
Death did its dreadful deed,
Stones lay cold upon that mead
Birds did not sing.
Flowers did not bring
Forth their fragrance
All was all calm and silence
The deep dark night,
In wait for the rising light
Of the brilliant Sun all bright.

Then the dawn
O, happy, happy morn
The tomb compelled
To open its door
For Jesus
To stay in it
No more

He is risen
He is risen
Glorious
Over us to reign.
The angels sing
Once again
Hallelujah he is risen
Hallelujah he is risen
Once again
Over us all to reign

He is risen indeed
Now, believe
And with him
Live
Now and ever more